ANCHOR BOOKS

OUT OF THIS WORLD

First published in Great Britain in 1993 by
ANCHOR BOOKS
1-2 Wainman Road, Woodston,
Peterborough, PE2 7BU

Foreword

Out of this World is a collection of poetical musings about the celebrated science fiction programmes that appear on our screens. It also delves into the mysteries surrounding our universe and the infinities of outer space.

Included are tributes to the Doctor that travels through time in a phone box and tales of Sam Beckett the Quantum physics scientist leaping in and out of time putting all wrongs, right.

I have chosen the poems which give a good portrayal of the characters in the science fiction programmes and those that delve deeply into the infinities of the unknown.

I hope this collection brings you as much pleasure reading as it did for me putting it together. Happy reading!

Michelle Abbott
Editor

Contents

Star Wars - The Evil and the Good

On the cinema screen, an explosion of light,
As mechanical *camels* begin to fight -
The men from earth - whose special power
means they need not run, or cower,
Away from such an alien breed,
For Jedi's have a special seed
Within, from ancient men - and wise,
Who valour and truth have learned to prize.
From cavern's depth, to stratosphere,
The pilots, and their foes career.
Darth Vader seems about to win -
Then vanquished, pays the price of sin,
Though battle scarred, our hero, with his sword of light,
Lives on, defending truth and right -
His father, turned evil, he had to slay,
So good could triumph on this bright, new day.
Amongst the stars, and on the earth,
Brave comrades all have proved their worth.

Margherita Smith

E - for Earth, Calling M - for Moon

E for Earth calling *M* for Moon,
Spread this message *arriving soon.*
Tell your sister planets and stars
We have set our sights on Mars!
Pass the word out there in space,
Watch - out for the Human Race!
We are Earthlings, we have powers,
Soon your secrets shall be ours.
Hear! O Planets, lost in Space,
We are of the Human Race.
We have conquered land and sea,
So, *watch out*, Eternity!
Neptune, Saturn, Pluto, too,
We have set our sights on you!
Jupiter, with your fifteen Moons,
Soon you shall hear different tunes.
Hark! O Mercury, Venus too,
We have not forgotten you.
E for Earth, calling *M* for Moon,
Spread the word, *Arriving Soon!*

Shirley Frances Winskill

Blade Runner Replicant

My beautiful but beautiful
Most desirable replicant
Your kind allowed no earthly home
From space you all have flown
Sent on to hunt them blown
Your friend's killed with utmost skill
No thrill then unto me
That's not your lover's will
Whom I've kiss no life to end
Other than takest with lover's friend.

Most Beautiful of all replicants
More desirable than human form
now I have created but a storm
So Blade Runner, run, run, run
Always in life your gun
With will you have shown
Your life power full grown
But now is your final hours
Blade Runner coming for your power
The golden rule ultimately broken
Your life without a token.

Lovely replicant, Oh lovely replicant,
Takest my hand
For let us run
For all we can
If we are not in time
Our lives will go blank
Because we two replicants.

E T Ward

The Six Million Dollar Man

Would commander Steve Austin stay on course,
He enlisted in the United States Air Force,
For his ambition to be an astronaut he fought,
As a NASA pilot his space wish he got.

His shuttle came crashing to the ground,
Where Steve Austin's lifeless body was found,
His arm and legs were smashed badly too,
He was almost left for dead 'til bionics came through.

Norad built him up with new eye, arm and legs,
Now for Steve the special agents help oscar begs,
Steve now bionic, smart and very strong,
He runs like a car with atomic fuel range long.

The Commander's eye can see all for miles,
The love of his friends with achievements smiles,
So Commander Austin now fights for your rights,
The friends you have can help you through the night.

Margaret Scott

Warp Factor

Captain Kirk I love your curls,
but you have kissed too many girls.
Mr Spock I'd eat your ears -
don't make me wait for seven years.
Superman's a pompous pain,
he can keep his Lois Lane.
Lister's just a hologram
and Rimmer's no renaissance man.
Doctor Who is out of time,
Blake and Avon past their prime.
Dan don't dare and Gordon's flash,
Batman's fat and Han *will* crash,
Thunderbirds! (I cannot look)
and Spiderman can sling his hook.
Heroes all through time and space
Aged hunks called home to base.

Susan Mayer

The War of the Worlds

Who could predict,
What would occur,
Strange objects falling,
Gliding through the air,
You then rise from the ground,
Like the devil from hell,
Our weapons are useless,
They can't pierce your glass shell,
You came to Earth,
With one thing in mind,
Overtaking our planet,
Destroying mankind.
Buildings are falling,
There's fire all around,
People are hiding,
They darn't make a sound,
As day becomes night,
Then night becomes day,
There's one last hope,
We can only pray.
Suddenly there's silence,
Then comes a sound,
We look, as your spaceships,
Crash to the ground.
You all wer destroyed,
It was hard to believe,
You were killed by the germs,
In the air that we breath.

S P Close

Crystal

Fountains of inspiration, thoughts rising, falling,
Tangible,
Intangible as they are grounded,
Without water,
Earth's barren
As a laughing life with a tear,
Touching you,
you will not be near;
Skittish, rolling on, in Summer,
A tangerine-in-suns,
Ballet dancing,
Balancing the light.
Winter, and you crystallize frozen,
Multifaceted, still as night,
I meditate
The ebb and flow of tides,
The Moon's mystery
The capture, the unfolding
Of your beauty.

Sue Osborne

Dimensions

There is the left side
the right side
and the side
down the middle
no this is not a riddle.

The Earth is one
round shape
but it has a side
that it tries to hide

All those we try
to enter it would
find it dimly lit
this is called the third dimension
I forgot to mention.

The twilight zone
where people vanish
or come home
were they simply
lost in space?

The outer limits
of deep space, make
the UFO give chase
we will all make haste.

Wendy L Barber

The Visionary

(Dedicated to Gene Roddenberry)

The man looked around him and his heart was saddened,
To hunger, disease and death man was hardened.
So he looked into the future and what did he see?
A vision of what mankind could be.

He saw peace on Earth, good will to all men,
And wondered at what it would be like to live then.
He saw ships that travelled through the stars,
Visiting planets near and far.

He saw friendships and loves that knew no boundaries -
Deep and abiding, long cherished memories.
He saw a caring for all, a willingness to share,
A giving of all, and more, that all could spare.

The man looked around him and his heart was saddened,
But remembering the visions his heart was gladdened.
For they gave him hope of what could be,
Even though he would not be there to see.

Christine Jones

Kray Fish

How does Lister with wit survive the only Human on the ship,
What life has Rimmer but intellect the hologram on a trip,
Why did the Red Dwarf's ship's cat evolve so human but stay so cool,
Where did Robot Kryton come from and why is Rimmer such a fool,
When did the Kray Fish sex change to Holly A Zippy Do Da Day.

How the Smeg will Lister hope to succeed in passing on his genes,
What Smeggin chance has Arnold Rimmer just to work out what it means,
Why will Cat hunt in vain because the ship's log listed the Kray Fish,
Where is true intelligence if to serve is Kryton's only wish.
When will the Knight on White Charger let the beautiful Holly Play.

How well does Lister reflect the future frozen humans in space,
What would be worse if Rimmer was the Zenith of the human race,
Why should felines be happy if Red Dwarf's ship's cat had pride of place,
Where will robots be in a thousand years will they have Kryton's grace,
When the Kray evolves to Holly swimming through space to show the way.

J D Scott

Quantum Leap: Dr Sam Beckett

Enter the life of one
Dr Sam Beckett
A man swept along
By the perilous mists of time.
Masked
By a relatively
Alien host
He continues his masquerade
Imprisoned
Between lifetimes,
Trapped between souls.
A prisoner of progression,
A traveller of technology.
He rides the lightning
Braving the unknown
And flexing the cords
Of humanity and time
Into one positive string of events
He utilises the power of the future
To rectify the misused power of the past.
A thousand personas he portrays
Yet woven through each personality
Remains a thread of his true self:
The saviour of souls
The prince of personas
The prophet of progression.

David McNamee (12)

Dr Sam Beckett

There's television, day and night,
Channelled, cable, satellite,
News and sport and travel shows,
Wildlife, games and goodness knows
How many other kinds of ways
To glut your nights, surfeit your days
With facts and figures, which inform
Until your brain whips up a storm.

I watch TV for relaxation,
Entertainment's revelation,
So my choices, to escape
From cold and boredom and red tape
Are adventures, timed and dated,
When Beckett is reincarnated.
I Quantum Leap each Tuesday night
With Doctor Sam - a wrong to right.
To spin the wheel of history
is this man's bitter destiny.
Repeatedly, he must endure
This fate, for which there seems no cure.
Only Al the hologram,
Extends his hand to exiled Sam.
Jousting to repeal the past,
Wishing each leap to be the last.
His only prayer, his only aim,
is to return to whence he came.
To harvest home, deserving peace.
Will his journeys never cease?
Oh boy! How I hope he'll keep
Making one more Quantum Leap.

Eileen Denham

Star Trick - The Next Generation

Now first of all there's Captain Jean-Luc Pickle Egg
No let's not be cruel he can't help his head.
How he tells Data 'full speed ahead'
Now Data's another matter for sure.
A real Mr Know it all.
What's he made from again.
A bit of metal and an implant of men.
Commander Riker, he's our man.
If Willy can't do it no-one can.
A real ladies man for sure.
For Willy Boy there is no cure.
Dr Crusher, a female doctor in more lights than one.
She's always there on call.
With her little digital.
Do they really need her likes.
Or is she just there to help the medicine go down.
Going down reminds me of Geordi La Forge.
When everyone else is sure their done for.
Geordi with visors aglow takes over the whole show.
Does he take off his visor at night.
Now that would set the show alight.
Lieutenant Worf, a warrior true.
I would not like to be stuck in a turbolift with him, how about you.
Animal magnetism, he's put to a shot.
With all that make up, no wonder he moans, doesn't he get hot.
Councellor Troy, she's the only one who knows what's going on.
She's just so depressed, she's the only one to read the script
for so long
Her last word will be 'Full speed ahead. Let's go home and
straight to bed.'

Chris and Dawn Biddle

Star Trek's Commander Data

On board the new Starship Enterprise.
It comes to me as no surprise,
That the one women find so charming,
So innocently disarming.
Is the android Commander Data,
Whose birthplace was Omicron Theta.

For though he's strong and superior,
He's never held in awe.
For that special gentle nature is always on show.
An unlikely sex symbol he may be,
But it's so very plain to see.
That with no attempt to persuade or cajole,
He wins the ladies over heart and soul.

So could a being capable of invoking such devotion,
Truly be devoid of all emotion?
Or could it possibly be,
He feels in a way that's just different from you and me.
For one lady appeared to have captured his heart.
But he and the lovely Tasha by cruel fate were destined to part.

Linda McGrath

Illusions

A blank screen, though the sounds of traffic linger -
Evidence of television after death?
Perhaps we had been sleeping all these years,
The haunting pictures sent out as lost dreams
When our own failed, after machines took over?

Little things move, like shock waves after gunfire,
The ordinary lies in wait; grey, speckled light
Sizzles, we strain our eyes as faced with smoke,
Wait to see clearly through this one blind eye,
Distrusting the familiar; grope towards
The emptiness where our small histories end

The width of a small room away, our losses
Suddenly apparent, rifled imaginations
Disguised as scenery in bed-sitting rooms;
We stand up slowly, prepare to reassess
Years of poor illustrations, sketch our lives,
Draft alibis in air until a hat

Follows the slipstream of a slim cigar
And glasses seeing nothing, a moustache
Hangs around with them, fading to announce
The Invisible Man, The End: we disappear.

Martyn Halsall

The Ballad of Blake

Down on the surface of Cygnus Alpha Five,
Rebellion is brewing,
Black patched Tarrant has just arrived.
In his pursuit ship stewing.

This was inspired by only one man,
Mutoids inwardly quake,
For in skin tight white slinks Servalan,
And cries, 'Tarrant, get me Blake.'
But they'll never catch him, they'll never make him break,
One man speaks for freedom and that one man is Blake.

Blake heads up a crew of seven
Cally, Villa, Gan,
Genna, and ships computer Zen,
Hostile Avon computer man,

Strike at brutal federation might
Universal dictator
By racing round a disused building site
Or on the airfix *Liberator*
The set may be wobbling but his firm heart will not shake,
He holds true to freedom, the rebel Roj Blake.

Wearing brown or Lincoln green
In a leather jerkin
Sinister wiring and vicious polystyrene
Could not unnerve him.

What did he fear to make him flit
And leave us to disaster
Was it outrageous acting or outfits
Or weapons made of plaster
Never did he flinch or fail when freedom was at stake
Until the third series of *Blakes Seven* without Blake.

Tracey O'Leary

Ultimate Hero

It was the prize you know, that caught my eye,
I couldn't lie, I'd rather die.
A poem it said, 'na' that ad be gud'
And so it should, well then it would.
About a hero on the box,
Who's good with locks and jumps off rocks.
He's got a crew, they're all around,
Don't make a sound we could be found.
Throws out orders like the boss,
Don't eat that moss and fetch my hoss!
He's got a ship, it's lightning fast.
It has no mast, but it's never last.
They roam around the biggest sea,
From A to B always free.
Meet the people from other lands,
Learn their thoughts and all their plans.
Mix amongst them, get to know
Who they'll fight and overthrow.
Diplomatic *watch your back*
Fake security then attack.
His jobs protector of the weak,
Fight the strong and save the meek.
Guess the name of my hero
Not Captain Scarlet or Captain Nemo.
he's not an actor from some old soap,
Earning money for old rope.
He's not nasty or a burke.

The ultimate hero is *Captain Kirk*.

S Nicholson

Thunderbirds

(Respectfully dedicated to Marjorie Crossley (nee Abson) who kindly bought me my first office typewriter.)

'Calling International Rescue, come in please.'
- Thunderbirds five, four, three, two, one, are indeed go, every time -
If only we could do, and be likewise -
No mission is ever too dangerous for them -
No task is ever too small -
Although they are all only puppets -
We can never both equal and therefore, surpass
Their continuous fortitude -
As yet
If only The Tracy Family
Their Associates
And their Fleet were real -
Mankind itself would surely survive vastly more worldwide
crises of any possible descriptions
So where on earth is the drawing board?

Michael Denholm Hortus Stalker

The Martian

Do you remember when we met that man,
who came from outer space?
He was eight feet tall, with bright green skin
and he had a funny face.

Imagine how we looked to him,
Mohicans, bobs and crops.
It must have seemed chaotic to him,
Our Ambulance men, Firemen and Cops.

Do you remember how he didn't stay long,
how he got back in his ship?
He shook our hand, as he wished us luck,
and then zoomed off rather quick.

Eve Chapman

The Main Source to Star Wars

Star Wars is a trilogy
with so much ability
it's a make believe world,
in it is war, love and comedy
there has been no other
with so much cover.
Luke was a pupil
Hans was a pirate,
Lea was a princess
they all became rebels.
Chewie, R2D2 and C3PO in tow
their only goal,
to see Darth Vader in a black hole
empire destroyed.
Rebels united
good and evil fight all the way
Obi Wan and Yoda are there to have a say.
The aliens and worlds which are created
are futuristic and not dated.
So stay with the Main Source
and be at one with the *Force*.

Karen Anne Henderson

Let's Beam Down and Join the Fun

The Starship Enterprise and it's crew
are travelling to find strange worlds new
Through the black void of space to soar.
To go where no man has gone before.
There's Captain Kirk, (Jim to his friends)
His sense of duty never ends.
In engineering there is Mister Scott
Who'll give the engine all he's got.
Doctor McCoy, who's known as *Bones*
Works tirelessly and seldom moans.
Lieutenant Ohura will communicate,
She'll try her best at any rate.
The ship will be guided to any realm
With Messrs Chekov and Sulu at the helm.
For logic then there's Mister Spock
Science Officer of Vulcan stock.
With this crew and many more
Lets visit worlds we can explore
But watch for Klingons on the way
And from your mission do not stray.
Now set your phasers on to stun
And let's beam down and join the fun.

James Michael Doolan

A Space Odd Essay

I thought I'd give a call to Doctor Who
Time warped enquiries could not get me through.
I walked in cow fields with much on my mind,
I suffered encounters of the turd kind.
I travelled where no man had gone before,
By treading in fresh snow outside my door.
My bride was moon struck when she married me,
Now she thinks she's wed to Alien Three.
People in wheat fields study magic rings
Way in the distance a late Cuckoo sings.
After doing the rounds in late night bars,
My pink elephant's changed to men from Mars.
A huge giant from space squashed our earth flat,
The Flat Earth Society, drank to that.
The most intricate space probe ever led,
Went whizzing round a politician's head.
The probe had a brainstorm and fell to ground,
Its last message to base read *nothing found.*

Alex S Haines

Mission Impossible

Aboard the Star Ship Enterprise
Were Kirk and Spock and Scottie
The Starlog showed directions to
The Planet Purple Spottie!

They proceeded to the Neutral Zone
At warp speed and a half
Kirk was busy at the flight deck
Checking every single graph.

His eyes were turning redder
There was anguish on his face
He cried, 'Spock, can't you find it?
For against time I must race!'

Spock searched the whole ship over
Looking for the *smallest room*
At long last he located it
Beside the engine room.

Jim Kirk could wait no longer
To the toilet he did run
The crewmen of the Enterprise
Thought Stars Wars had begun!

But Spock then reassured them
'Captain Kirk will not be long
He is very boldly going
Where no other man has gone!'

Marjorie C Edgar

Aboard the Enterprise

Children, eyes glued to the box do not heed my words,
They are at one with what they watch, Myself they have not heard.
Starship Enterprise speeds on, Commander, Captain Kirk.
Intrepid spaceman whom they know, his duty will not shirk.
Special crew have served him long, been through such a lot.
The best known one of all of them, is Alien Mister Spock.
He has computer for a brain, much logic is in there.
Helping Commander with skill so great, none else can compare.
Flying higher than before to places yet unseen.
Risking everything to go, where no-one else has been.
My children act so terrified as awful things they find.
Creatures which if there in flesh, would blow their tiny minds.
Scottie, Spock and others will simply be beamed down,
Swiftly deal with objects, plus all problems found.
Job is done, they're beamed back up, kids sigh with relief,
Spock is now reporting on the mission to his chief.
Captain Kirk sits quietly, then simply nods his head,
Signals to the crew, 'Well done' though not a word is said.
Passing through the atmosphere they other planets seek
Programme ends, the caption says, 'Remember, watch next week,'
My children very gradually, come back into life's' sway,
But in further seven day's again they'll fly away.
While they go adventuring, I'll get on with my work.
They'll be on Starship Enterprise, Commander, Captain Kirk.

Barbara I Goode

Switcheroo Doctor Who

Behold the Universe so sublime,
Man's many Questions never subside.
Doctor Who, why travel Space and Time,
Is it from Now that you hide.
Let Cause and Effect baffle Mankind,
Seek Eternal Now and Peace of Mind.
Switcheroo Doctor Who,
Pooh-pooh the hullabaloo.

Paul Corrigan

Guess Who!

Time and space stop for only one
From Planets, Moons even the Sun,
He's a remarkable man this lord of time
Who travels through space with his dog K9.
The Tardis is both his work and home
From whatever part of time he chooses to roam,
He goes to planets we didn't know were there
And battles with creatures we wouldn't dare.
From Cybermen to Darleks
With their awful ways and dirty tricks,
To exterminate People they try to do
But they are always saved by *Doctor Who.*

Angela Peall

Star Tracks of V'ger

- V'ger is the Voyager space probe in a Star Trek film. The Voyager series carry gold records with voices and other sounds of Earth on them -

Rays shall show what told

As we, that star's left, go gold . . .

Page shall blot dearly when
Roars the ears on them:
Matter's going round of the tongues
Scanned in her draw-in:

We still remembered, then.

Brendan Guy

Star Wreck

I was getting out my head, smoke was getting in my eyes
Then I found I couldn't get up off the floor
Lieutenant Uhuru appeared and told me to arise.
Did I dream it up or beam up - I'm not too sure.

On the bridge I said, 'Hi,' to Captain Kirk and Spock
To be told I was now one of the crew
Our mission - to seek out life on lumps of rock
And sell them Yankee culture - oh, and something useful too.

So we roamed the skies in Enterprise, hairstyles set to stun
Like a hippy commune in acid-powered flight
Our minds all in warp-drive, having so much fun
Regular nebula wanderers high as kites.

Suddenly there's Klingons in front of us
Klingons up our ass, Klingons everywhere I glance
The captain shouts, 'Let's head 'em off at the pass.'
I look again and the captain's Jack Palance!

Bones is Henry Fonda, Sulu's Michael Caine!
Spock is cracking walnuts on his ears!
There's aliens on the bridge gargling with champagne
Uhuru's singing *Tracks of my Tears.*

Smoky sings on as the smoke drifts away
The digital display flashes *red alert* red
This space/time travel cosmic thing's ok
But safer getting out your head than getting out of bed.

Rod Eyre

Star Trek

Generation to Generation
We've grown up with them
Throughout the nation
Captain Kirk says
'Beam me up Scotty'
Aye, Aye, Captain, but you must be
Potty
Mr Spock with his pointed ears
says ' It's illogical captain'
But have no fears
The Enterprise and all its crew
Will win the day and see you through
So once again Kirk's quest is done
And once again the battle is won.

Stephen Richards

The Flying Phone Box

Doctor Who is a most unusual chap
he flys round the earth in a phone box,
with lots of whimsical characters
most of them wearing odd socks.
Exterminate the Daleks all cry
as they slide around looking quite ominous,
with poker like things sticking out like arms
ready to kill on sight if it's obvious.
The Doctor can move into orbit
either backwards in time or then on,
he knows about all kind of weapons
or even an old fashioned bomb.
Sometimes the Doctor is ancient
other times he looks very young,
with the long woollen scarf around his neck
his long-johns he makes sure he's got on.
So if you feel like phoning someone
be careful the phone box you step in,
you might take off at a very fast pace
which will make you feel like a cretin.

Marjorie Mary Pearson

ET Goes Home

ET he wants to phone home,
But he lives so far away to use a phone.
He got left behind when visitors called,
They came to visit from outer space
And left in a hurry at a terrific pace.
Poor ET it was such a trial
He had come such a long way and was only a child.
He was frightened and so very sad,
Then from a house on earth he met a young lad.
He helped ET to go home with the help of his brother.
ET was so happy to be back with his mother.
Young ET said he would come back to visit,
So open your eyes and search up high
And look for their spaceship high in the sky.

Valerie Coulman

Doctor Who

I travel in my Tardis I am Doctor Who
You don't know me but I know you.
I can go back in time or forward you see
Chasing the master where ever he may be.
I've fought the Dragonyions and Darleks too
So I can protect the Earth for people like you.
See they all want to take over the planet Earth.
But I was born in a little house in Perth.
I've been locked in dungeons, prisons and Jails
And been touched, tied up, and laid on nails.
My travelling seems to be for ever and ever
But I will not give up never no never.
I have a travelling companion her name is Jane
She is the only thing that keeps me sane.
One fine day I will be able to rest
But until then I will keep doing my best.
So I am on my way again and take care
One day perhaps you'll wake up and I'll be there.

M Stephenson

Quantum Mechanics and Doctor Sam Beckett

The trials and tribulations of a soul
Plunged into a body at a certain point in its life
Not knowing what may happen in the next second
An exponent of the theory of quantum mechanics
The man who performs quantum leaps, Doctor Sam Beckett.

From one body to another, male or female
Within a time span of his own earth years
Taking on the trials that have befallen that life
In an endeavour to alter its course to a smoother path
Always facing the possibility in doing so, he may die.

Meanwhile, only the mirror reveals his new face
Life as a man, or woman, perhaps an African American
Sometimes rich, sometimes poor, whose trouble is very deep
Al, the hologram, trying to feed him new information
Oh boy, says Sam, facing a sticky situation after another leap.

In Sam's real time, there is Ziggy, the computer
Checking the course of events through Al, the hologram
Sam always hopes his turmoil will cease
And he will return to his own body, and life
Only then will he find, at last, perfect peace.

Robin Barker

Mission of Peace

Captain Kirk and all his crew
Set out to explore space.
To find new life beyond the stars
Besides the human race.

These very brave and fearless men
Left earth so far behind,
And many strange new planets sought
And new friends did they find.

They also made some enemies
Of men who thought they'd rule,
But Captain Kirk came out on top
Because he is no fool.

His crew and he sought peace for all,
No fighting evermore.
To teach the people love will rule,
Then hate flies out the door.

Gillian M Thomson

Doctor Who

Doctor Who? the next generation will say
They won't remember that remarkable day
When we were introduced to that time traveller in space,
Who travelled in a tele-transporter named
Tardis with no face.

The Doctor in question was a scientist
Who wanted to travel in time,
They met many strange creatures
Covered in horrible slime!
The most famous metal monster
Called a Darlek what a name!
Would exterminate at random
Anyone who wouldn't play their game.

There were toy replicas mass produced
Such was their success
Metal monsters with metal feelers
Who could zap with a press!
Each week the episode would end
Leaving you scared
The music would start,
Would the Doctor be spared!
Would he return to the time he knew well
Tune in next week to fall under his spell.

C Stocks

It's a Five Year Mission?

Captain Kirk, Mr Spock, Dr McCoy and crew are on the TV again.
I cannot but wonder when will this five year mission end?
With constant amazing dilemmas and deadly foes
They always succeed and survive and everybody knows!
Oh, Captain Kirk do you have to constantly plead, 'Beam me up Scotty?'
For our sanity's sake please stop, it's driving us all potty.
Mr Spock from Vulcan with pointed ears and so logical
Could you please tell me why you have to be so boring and methodical?
And Doctor McCoy, Ship's Medical Officer, Captain's friend and nicknamed Bones
You say again 'he's dead Jim' and I can only hear viewers' whimpers and groans.
Oh Star Trek, I wish you would end and not go on and on,
For I find myself crying with so much ease, 'Come on you Klingons!'

Jonathan Brewer

Doctor Who What One

An ordinary police box, with a blue light on top,
Open up a tiny door, peer inside, you'll get a shock.
What a great big tardis or travelling machine,
Oh what a lovely colour, was it blue, maybe green.
Dr Who would disappear into his tardis box,
He'd press dials and switches and undo great big locks.
He'd travel with assistant, to times long ago,
They would face all kinds of people, some they didn't know.
But every now and then the same ones would appear,
They were Daleks, it was them I used to fear.
The planets were made of cardboard, the people dressed in grey
The way they spoke in English was curious in a way,
But what never failed to amaze me, when Jon Pertwee met his
maker,

Was on the next episode, Dr Who was now Tom Baker.

M A Nixon

Don't Boldly Go

Never beam down with Mr Spock, Uhura or James T.
If they should ask for volunteers, always shout, 'Not me.'
Unless you are a regular upon the Enterprise,
to accompany the Away Team is always most unwise.
Before you've primed your phaser, to kill or just to stun,
You'll be a lump of smouldering dust, the odds are ten to one.
Bones will have scanned you with his instrument and with a face
set grim,
have turned to the assembled crew and said that, 'he's dead Jim.'
Mr Spock whilst looking fascinated at you, the pile of grit,
will have paraphrased his well known words, 'He's not life as we
know it.'
The same applies if your mother says that you're the Captain's son.
Just pack your bags and take off quick at speed warp factor one.

Pauline Brennan

Enterprising

'Oh Captain, answer Captain,'
Pleads Uhura to the planet below
She didn't know where the captain was -
He beamed down an hour ago.

'Poor Captain,' says McCoy to Spock,
'I'm afraid he must be dead.
He was armed when he went to the alien planet
But the jumper he wore was red.'

The captain shouts, 'Oh crew,' He says,
'Please rescue me quick or I'll die.
There are Klingons on the starboard bow -
Blow them out of the skies!'

'Oh Captain,' mocks the Klingon brute,
'You're in a bit of a spot
With nothing left to hide behind
But a meagre Styrofoam rock.'

'It's alright Captain!' shout the eager crew,
'You've had your bit of fun
We've blasted the ship with photon torpedoes -
The Klingons are on the run!'

'Oh Captain, my Captain!
The Klingons have upped and gone
The ship is sagging at the seams,
Our mission here is done.'

But 'Captain, oh Captain!'
Says Scotty, 'We cannot leave!'
'The engine canna take no more,
She's given her final heave!'

Kirsty Holland

The Void

The dwindling megaspace through which
The fleet starship has flown - on its mission
To explore new worlds or galaxies as their rich
And original states reveal the vast division
Still in culture that exists beyond this little Earth -
Remains the same illimitable void
That it has been since Time began.
Only Man's ingenuity has him up-buoyed,
Only Man's curiosity has not yet been outrun
By his complacency or his computered store
Of knowledge (still thought to be - at times - of little worth
Unless made useful for establishing democracy
After democracy or a loved-filled life of mirth
Or to down-trod a tyrant or some petty tyranny):
And only Man's plea for something new remains.

The void - it seems - will always be
Filled with that we'll never know:
And there'll be sufficient mystery
To keep this - and the next - generation on peak-time show.

S V Batten

Boldly Going into Sci-Fi TV

Phrases from my childhood,
Can still be heard now:
'Warp factor nine, Mr. Sulu,'
'There's Klingons on the starboard bow.'
Although I'm now much older,
Still I love to see,
Kirk, Spock and Co,
Boldly going into sci-fi tv.

It's rumoured that Prince Charles's a fan,
Jonathan Ross and Bill Clinton too,
Maybe it's illogical,
But that's how Star Trek affects you!

Patrick Hennessy

Red Dwarf . . .

There is a sitcom set in outer space,
Not Peckham, Railway Cuttings or other Earthly place.
Although television watchers in the know
Have said it's a futuristic *Steptoe.*
The *Red Dwarf* is a spaceship, now set adrift,
Its crew thrown together - they cannot work shifts.
They make each other paranoid -
Human, Hologram, Cat and Mechanoid.
On board there are in fact five,
Although Lister's the only one truly alive.
He's the human, who hails from Liverpool
The Cat is a creature gifted in cool.
Holly's the computer, supremely scatty,
Once played by Norman, now alias Hattie.
Kryten quotes in Binary language,
A mechanoid with human anguish.
Arnold J Rimmer is the hologram
Who likes *Reggie Wilson* (on Polygram?)
When alive he was a chicken soup vendor
Elvis sang the theme once - *Not* 'Return to Sender'.
Camille was good, she was a Pleasure Gelf,
The Inquisitor was *Thyself*
The boots of *Justice* atoned for sins,
But whatever happened to Lister's twins?
Surviving attack from a *Polymorph*,
There's still only one *Red Dwarf.*
Better Than Life, you know it's true,
'In Binary language, Sir, 2212!'

Angela White

A Dream in Space

Gazing into the night sky,
Little is visible to the naked eye,
But just imagine and dream,
Put yourself in the time machine.
Join the Doctor as his guest,
Go with him on his eternal quest.

Exciting, wouldn't it be?
Zooming around the galaxy.
Off into the unknown,
So far away from home.
A time traveller in space,
Meeting every conceivable race.

Visiting planets far and near,
Going to goodness knows where.
Daleks, Cybermen and other foe,
All of these we'd overthrow.
Make the universe a safe place,
Protect it all for the human race.

That is the ultimate goal.
Doctor Who's lifetime role.
And when he's tired of this,
He retires back into the Tardis.
Regeneration is his scheme,
Emerge anew to realise the dream.

Marina Hargreaves

The Millennium Falcon

In the deepest pit of space,
Worlds are turning faster,
Stars shoot in all directions,
A bright light streams across the sky.

The fastest hunk of junk,
Roars across the galaxy,
Dodging through asteroid storms,
Confronting the darkness of evil.

With Chewbacca and Hans Solo,
Manning the Falcon's controls,
They protect the rebels cause,
By destroying the evil forces.

Travelling through the solar system,
Passing multicoloured planets,
They're searching into space,
For freedom and for justice.

Philip May

Reminiscences From an Old Trekkie

I've watched Star Trek for many a year
To see dashing Captain Kirk, no blooming fears!
Mr Spock was the one for me with his *logic*
And his cute pointed ears!
Well the Star Ship Enterprise, journeyed for many years.
But alas, things started happening to the crew.
Admiral Kirk became pudgy and fat, and to get
Into his uniform he needed a cork screw!
Mr Spock's face was even more lined and
His *logic* was not up to scratch!
While Bones, looked as if *his bones* would
Soon need a sticking plaster patch!
Uhura started to look like somebody's mother!
And Scotty's Scot's accent seemed to be giving him bother!
So they pensioned them off and signed on another crew.
But Oh! for me they just wouldn't do!
For this Captain is a skinhead with no glamour at all!
And the rest are so mediocre they'd drive you up the wall!
And not a Mr Spock in sight!
So *Beam me up Scotty*, to some other planet!
And with any luck Mr Spock, might be there living on it!

Flora Divers

Captured

They came, they saw, they conquered
And captured a whole nation
With their lasers and phasers.

Captain Kirk was their leader.
Spock his right hand man.
McCoy led the way in the sick bay.

Through warp speed they travelled
To save innocents from enemy
Fought bravely on, with the mighty *Klingon.*

Beam me up Scottie, became the word of the day
Back to enterprise.
While Spock lacked emotion, an empire showed devotion.

From children to aged held in their sway
They will always be there, in space
It's their final frontier, for many a year.

Sheila Cole

Star Trek

To venture where no-one has before
Who could know what lies in store
From Earth they travelled though deep space
The Enterprise flew at a terrific pace.
Their mission to protect each civilisation
Of every planet within the Federation.
But their mission of peace do not always work
To verify that, just ask Captain Kirk.
Klingon warships would attack on a whim
And Kirk's survival would look rather slim.
But the Enterprise would conquer to save the Federation
And help make way for the next generation.

R Mickleburgh

Star Trek

Beam me up Scotty
On the Starship Enterprise,
You're a kind man
I can see it in your eyes
Show me how it is to feel
Weightless, timeless and unreal.
Daydreams form a small respite
Scoop me up into the night,
Wars are waging everywhere
There's a tension in the air.
Plants and life forms here are dying
Sadly the rain for earth is crying,
If those other worlds exist
Take me there instead of this.
On the Earth we've lost our grip
All's safe inside the saviour ship.

Elizabeth Casey

They Boldly Go

We've seen them again and again,
But watch each time they're repeated.
We delight in mysterious worlds,
And enemies, always defeated.

We know all the plots by heart,
And the crew all seem like family.
I'm sure we all have favourites
To whom we show our loyalty.

The Captain is one for the ladies,
As a youngster I found it a bore,
But now, much older, I envy them,
He is the one I adore.

The appeal of this crew is enduring,
Has lasted for many a year;
What a sadder, duller world this would be,
If they should disappear.

Kathleen Mann

Invasion of the Body Snatchers

Don't close your eyes! You'll drift off to sleep.
Trailing tendrils will sway and sweep
Down your wall to the arm of your chair,
Caressing your skin, stroking your hair.
A green, marrow, pod will split at your feet,
Secreting a scent, insidious and sweet,
Stealing your soul and draining your mind.
Cloning your form, as its tentacles wind
Tighter and tighter around your throat.
Your eyes will pop and your carcass bloat.
Hideous on your perfidious bier,
You realise too late, the Body Snatchers are here.

Jan Ferrierr

Boldly Going

The crew of the Star Ship Enterprise
How did they *Boldly Go?*
'Cos it just ain't proper English
And I would like to know
How they conversed with other Life
When they were much too slow
To learn their language properly
While they were down below.

And when they were Boldly Going
Did they ever stop to check
If they were on the Enterprise,
Or some other star ship's deck?
They were seldom where they ought to have been.
(That would make me a nervous wreck.)
But! they always got back safely
To continue on their trek.

Captain Kirk and Scotty
Have left the Expedition
But they pop up unexpectedly
In dubious condition,
As if they're still *Boldly Going*
Where no Man has gone before.
I suspect they'll be *Boldly Going*
For a hundred years, or more.

Lillian Parker

The Trouble With Yuppies

'Beam me up Scottie!' - came the call
From Captain James Kirk, Spock and all,
Who were down on the planet Yup,
Knowing the crew would beam them up.
'Warp Factor two, Mr Sulu please.'
Uhura coughed, then gave a sneeze,
'I think I've a cold in my head.'
'It's Yuppie 'flu!' - Mr Chekov said.
Bones gave them all a purple pill
To stop the crew from being ill.
'Exploring Yup was lots of fun,
But catching 'flu just isn't done!'
Spock shook his head in disbelief,
'To have green blood's such a relief,
A Vulcan can't catch Yuppie 'flu
No matter what I try to do.'
'For goodness sake!' - yelled Captain Kirk,
'This subject now begins to irk,
The Enterprise is going home
And nevermore the skies to roam.
We've wandered space and want no more,
And been where no man's gone before.
We will leave the Federation
To the *Next* (space) *Generation*!'

Diana H Adams

Captain Kirk

The Enterprise goes on its way
Entering danger day by day,
Never to know where its fate may lie
What is hiding there in wait to try and defeat Captain Kirk.

The Universe is vast and wide
No-one knows what is there inside
There appears to be something unknown
So he descends down to look around
And see what's to be found
When he is satisfied with what he sees
He'll say, 'Beam me up Scottie right away,'
He is projected to his ship to decide
Which way is best to tackle it.

Sharon Langham

Enter Enterprise

Star Trek with its crew so bold,
Science fiction as yet untold
Daring deeds, out there is space,
Surprises us, the human race.
Captain Kirk, and dear old Doc
Chekov, Scottie, and Mr Spock.
To go and do the deed they do
Gives inspiration to me and you
See the heavens as never before
Opens up the galaxy's door
Peace is what they aim to keep,
Way, way out in the deep,
            Universe!
Where no man has ever gone,
In the blue, black space beyond.
Thrill us Star Trek with your crew,
So that we feel there with you.
I am Kirk, you are Spock,
Mark is Chekov
            Who is Doc!

Phyllis Casewell

Star Trek

Captain Kirk runs the Enterprise,
With help from Mr Spock,
They might get a surprise,
They might get a shock,
On their journeys through space
They see lots of different things.
Going from place to place,
With all the fun and heartbreak it brings.
Riding through the stars,
They sometimes get attacked,
By Clingons from afar.
Other creatures might attack.
If anyone gets hurt,
Then Doctor McCoy will always do his best.
He'll try his hardest,
Giving the patient plenty of rest.
Space is normally a tranquil place,
With peace and serenity.
But when you come face to face,
With the Enterprise you'll see,
There are many adventures,
And things happening,
It won't be serene
It'll be the most exciting place you've ever been.

J Y Darts

Blake's Mission

Holds no boldness here -
we go because we are driven.
A game of stepping stones
with space in between
does not kindle any thrill
or satisfaction.

Stars stare with endless vacancy
and we wonder where the riches went,
along with the dream.
Inflight silence sometimes shattered
by a scream:
memories of death reliving the sudden
bright blood of torn hearts,
the black vacuum of promises betrayed.

Planetfall brings plunder
and a chance to kill again,
shoulder to shoulder, our trust on a hair-trigger,
mowing down men.
We smile as primeval as dinosaurs,
lasering our way to extinction.

It is a long narrow road
with no end.
And no sides.

Steve Bowkett

Alien Nations

We called them sponge heads, what a cheek
This people really are unique
They came from Tenton, where they were enslaved
A life of freedom is what they craved.
George Francisco, his wife Sue
Their son Butch, daughter Emily too
They made their lives really happy on earth.
And Susan was overjoyed when she gave birth
They made a human friend, Skyes was his name
He was also a detective, they were both the same
Human and Fentoness, united fighting crime
No over seers here, not this time
They're made a life, happy and free
So humans please except them and let them be.

Ellen Potter

Skywalkers

Oh why do you hide away under that mask?
Cause it's safe,
Metal can't cry but it can't laugh either.

Half man, half machine - I'm sorry to see you stuck,
Can't feel anything anymore; can't love us,
Are we really that bad or does it just hurt too much?

I know you're still in there Jedi Knight,
The man the emotion the soul,
That's the Power that's the Force
And you've locked it all away underneath pain.

Feel the energy flow - it's so evil on the Dark Side,
You know you can't share it and it can't love you back;
It won't make you feel any better it won't understand.

Your metal flesh could rust, it could melt away;
If you want to be free, free to feel the whole Universe,
It's not too late - you don't fool me Schizophren,
Two inside one Black on White.

And there's so much good, don't waste it,
Even for a minute look on life;
Feel life breath life, through your own skin my Father,
I mean we're all prisoners.

Can't you see everyone's trapped, stuck inside space inside time,
Everyone's weak and alone,
Don't be so proud Dad we all make mistakes.

If only you'd look at the stars,
They're everyone's forever,
You could never control them
So my Lord why don't you join life?

Eleanor Tracey

Doctor Who Bliss

I remember the Hartnell years,
Pertwee, and Tom Baker.
They seemed to make the Universe
A little more safer.

Fighting Daleks and strange monsters,
Across the land.
Always on adventure,
In the incredible Tardis.
Facing danger and evil.
Always winning, always bringing excitement
Of Doctor Who, bliss.

Kenneth Mood

USS Enterprise

They rush through space, at warp speed,
To passing stars they pay no heed.
To planets flung far and wide,
They took us along for the ride.
Their allotted mission, to find new life,
Many a quest brought trouble and strife.
But our brave Captain James Kirk,
His starfleet duties, he didn't shirk.
Helped by logical First Officer Spock, and crew
Uhura, Chekov, Scottie, McCoy and Sulu.
The Starship Enterprise, home to many more,
All bound by a common need to explore.
Uhura, receives and sends messages through space,
Chekov and Sulu, navigate and set the pace.
Doctor McCoy, in charge of sickbay,
Their aches and pains he takes away.
Then there's Mr Scott, Chief Engineer,
When all goes dark, he's always near.
Captain and Spock, go down to see,
If sighted planet had water or tree.
To return they say 'Beam us up Scottie,'
And there I'd sit, eating my tea.
Now Kirk and Co; no longer roam the stars,
They stay on Earth, and ride in cars.
The Next Generation have taken over,
Picard and Warf, now Star Trekking rovers.

Janet Dovaston

Seeing Stars

I'll take my Star Wars pencil and my Star Wars pad
and write a Star Wars poem 'cos I'm Star Wars mad -

Star Wars is great Star Wars is groovy
going by the blurb it's one helluva movie.

Man's reached for the stars and walked on the moon
better queue at the cinema it's coming soon,

Sit in the dark and stare at the screen
could this be the best thing you've ever seen,

Sweet Princess Leia she's a peach
but she's light years out of my reach.

Luke Skywalker he's my hero
not to mention C3PO,

R2D2 bleeps and is cute
but that Darth Vader is a nasty brute.

Never fear tho' good will surely win
don't expect surprises in a plot so thin

It's got a really forceful slogan *May the Force be with you*
go on force yourself to say it it's the trendy thing to do

come out starry-eyed and get it here
your very own Star Wars souvenir.

There's Star Wars tee-shirts and Star Wars soap
no down-to-earth product has much of a hope

can't wait for the sequel what will it be
Carry on Star Wars just you see.

PS:
now the Empire Strikes Back well don't you know
the saga will continue, I told you so.

Dalek Capture

The noise from the Tardis vibrates in Jo's ears,
She doesn't know how long they've travelled, but it felt like years.
The Doctor appears out of nowhere, with his newest face,
A long, long scarf and Jelly Babies, he wonders where's this place.

A barren land of sand, no water and no plants,
Not a thing there stirred, except the ants that march,
Across the barren land a building solidly sits.
So they both set off, the Doctor keeps his wits.

He knows that somewhere danger lurks,
He's worried about Jo in case she gets hurt,
His loyal assistant, but she knows not to ask,
Where it is they're going, or what's the next task.

Once in the building, they move along with caution,
The building is in ill repair, and everywhere's corrosion.
They don't know where they're going, they're totally at a loss.
The Doctor looks through the window and whispers, Stavross.

Jo doesn't know who Stavross is, but the look on the Doctor's face,
Tells her that whatever he is, he's not good for the human race,
From behind them a mechanical voice, shouts out halt,
They turn round slowly, knowing full well they've been caught.

Mechanical dustbins with wheels and human brains,
The Doctor knows can destroy and inflict great pain,
Jo collapses as she knows death will become her fate.
The Dalek's point and then they shout, exterminate, exterminate.

Lisa Jayne Bronger

The War of the World

It followed a railway line,
Then saw the sand,
And landed behind the mountain peaks
They were from that planet
Near a twinkling star,
We call the Sun.
Two lovers gazing at the starlit sky,
First saw that trembling light,
Then like the snake's forked tongue
The space ships shot forth
An orange flame,
Turning everything to dust,
When people were praying
In that church
Lit up with a ghastly crimson glow.
The creatures fell out of the sky
Killed by poison air,
God had answered
Their prayer.

R Owen

Just Who are You?

Just like an idol - stood you there,
proud and tall yet,
the balance shifts the clouds gather
and blackened stinging rain rips your naked body apart.

Through all of your disguises I saw truth,
through all of fantasies inventions you triumphed,
just how much truth is contained in your creator's mind,
you, who are you? just who . . .

Davros in his weakness lacked truth,
seadevil's like lemmings in reverse from the sea,
and that now distant blue box of escapism
fades, trapped in the archives of wise producers heads.

Seven faces one personality
seems like you epitomise people who
in travel's such as mine must some day face the master
and even my doctor won't tell me what's wrong with me.

We travelled a long way from first schooldays,
tiptoed through primary school, walked down the
early teens and erupted out of school to face my
own personal enemies and that one I could never quite see
but now see clearly every morning's break.

Oh doctor as noble as any character invented,
return now in form of face number eight,
mould your mind into mine and although it's only rented,
I'll live as Doctor who until destiny meets that preordained date.

Paul Cornell

Captain Kirk

Boldly kissing whom no man his kissed before,
Going inexhaustibly through the darkness,
Touching lips
And lifting the many hearts
Within and beyond the final frontier.

His five year mission
To seek out the old delights,
To voyage the unknown ways of women
For whom love lay as distant as the stars.

From out of nowhere,
Transported into their emotions at warp-speed
And to leave again
On an Enterprise only rarely glimpsed.

To contradict that life is not as we know it,
Kissing fills the empty channels,
Communicates deep into the neutral zone.

Kissing his way through the galaxies
Not as a Federation Commander
But as a man.
A man lifted by the experience of leadership.

A man known among the bliss of unforgotten pleasures
As Kirk,
Captain James Kirk.

G Jeffery

The Death of McCoy

Mighty Nimrod burning red black world of the evil dead
darkened race with Demon souls reaching our world through black holes,
coming from the end of times searching space for evil minds
spreading evil creed and lies Captain Kirk against which vies,
knotted from his head to knees by malignant space disease
brave McCoy once more ships out 'pon a one one way trip no doubt.
James T Kirk his comrade grieves as his fleet for Nimrod leaves
Klingon Captain Klug Grrrraaakk follows Kirk 'pon Nimrod track,
Klug views Kirk as deadly foe who has caused him much dark woe
Kirk must die at Klingon hands as the Kling Empire expands.
Klug must conquer Nimrod red planet of the evil dead
race of sick and evil swine must to Klug their power resign,
Kirk too plans to hold control over creatures black of soul
horned with teeth of rabid grip crossing time in demon ship,
ageing Kirk now grey of head weary that he'll soon be dead
shoots towards red evil globe silver Federation probe.
As it quick through black space drones in its hulk lies Doctor Bones
guiding probe to Demon sphere due to space plague lacking fear
as it enters inner space home of fiery Demon race,
skin bespecked with deadly spots shrivels crackles fries and rots
on this Hellish one man trip laser fire has hit his ship
burnt its way through leadened hull into kidneys, spleen and skull.

Stuart Murray

The Next Generation - Episode Haiku

The Enterprise in danger
Everyone will die
Who will save us?

Danger, another plot complication
The Klingons have arrived!

This episodes Okuda Device -
Triolic waves?
Data wins!

Anon (7)

Doctor Who

Doctor Who, Doctor Who,
Never goes to the loo.
He travels in a *TARDIS*
Which to fly quite hard is.
He fights Daleks and Cybermen,
Zygons, Vegans and Dustbin men,
And sometimes has to face his most deadly enemy of all,
The Master,
Who's a complete and total utter b . . .
Frantic chases down corridors,
Behind the sofa, here be horrors!
'I'll just reverse the polarity of the neutron flow,
It's the only way to save the Universe, Jo.'
So If you're feeling blue,
Put on a smile and watch Doctor Who.

John Smith

Saurian Major

It seems to me their souls live on,
As secret whisperings flow and rise,
through slender fissures
of this sunbleached earth.
Drowned out from hearing by the deafening noise
of winds, roaring unhindered across
this barren wasteland.

I listen helpless to their damning accusations,
One, then many voices flood my mind.
Relentless, persuasive, theirs the only sound
in this never ending silence.
Tainting and gouding, urging me forward,
guiding me to where it will end
and I shall rejoin them.

Lindsey Jayne Shelton

Dust of Old Saturdays

Thing I sense behind sofa
dead cats clawed must be
my son hiding from some
ultrahorror out of Doctor Who,
has to be, nothing else.
Certainly he's long grown-up, gone,
nor speaking when he visits.
But his real self's still
hiding safe there waiting like
Timelord to ambush Dalek Dad.

Steve Sneyd

Illusion

The substance and the shadows
Nestle side by side,
Like buildings through a window
Seen at eventide:
There is a slender difference
Between the views perceived
And the airy half-truths
Of the things believed;
And though you search forever,
Seldom will you find
The Truth that hides its secrets
In the depths of the mind.

Joan Croft

Inner Feelings

The wind stops, no birds fly,
In this world of suffering strain and stress,
It would be agreeable to look upon a kindly face,
Who's heart would understand the others' fears
And graduate, as a substitute peer.
Whilst struggling with ones agonising thoughts,
Another human could be a support,
Someone who does not criticise or condemn,
Is this to be found in women or in men?
All should be equal whether grand or poor,
But it's understanding the inner soul that opens the door,
Not only seeing the outer shell,
Trying to cope with life,
But understand the inner conflict
That causes all the strife.

Anna Parkhurst

The Ghost of Children

I am the Ghost of Children
That likes to glee
I float around
For them to see,
Boo Hoo come play
I hear a scream
How I laughed,
Boo Hoo come play
As they scream again
I laughed so much
I bumped my head
But now I must rest
As I do my best
I was just nodding off
When I hear
Someone say
Boo Hoo come play
All I could do was scream
It was the children
Dressed like me
Now I know not to glee.

T Salt

The Ghost of Lady Thalia

Don't go into the haunted wood.
You may never come out, there's evil about
The Ghost of Lady Thalia roams
With blood on her face
She shrieks and moans
Her hair is black, her eyes are green,
She moves alone with feet unseen,
Thalia wears a red dress
Which touches the ground
There's a sword in her hands,
That she swings around,
I see you Lady Thalia,
This is how it should be
For I am the Ghost of the man
You murdered in Fourteen, Fifty Three.

I was your lover, my misfortune,
We often met by the light of the moon,
But you did not love me, I was your fool,
You only used me, that was so cruel,
Then one night, as I slept in your bed
You came into the room, and cut off my head.

Stephen L Freeman

Marius is Careful

The Doctor and Leela start to shrink
And Marius is careful not to blink.
The pair are put in a syringe
Slowly they start to spin.
As they enter the Doctor's skin.

Peter Evans

Star Man

This man was a wonder, who came from afar,
His home was a planet his home was a star,
He came into being into a woman's life
Who had already known love as someone's wife.

He entered her home and through videos of the past,
Went from baby to manhood, the pace was so fast!
You could hear the bones growing, you could hear the skin stretch,
There was no way of knowing just follow the next sketch.

The woman screamed and finally he stood tall,
Looking exactly like her husband, like the photograph on the wall.
They talked and he told her he meant her no harm,
He had come from a planet, full of wonder, full of calm.

They became friends and decided to go for a car ride,
They stopped at a cafe where a dead deer he spied.
He gently stood over it as on the car boot it lay,
It miraculously moved slowly, then quickly ran away.

His powers were endless and so he told her of his love,
As he had little time to stay, he must return above.
The woman had always longed for a child of her own,
He loved her and told her she would never be alone.

He gave her a small sphere, in remembrance of his stay,
He said their child would inherit powers far beyond his day,
His only sadness was he had to return to space,
So she took him, sadly to the very place,
Where the powerful space ship dipped lightly on the sand
Whisked, away her Star Man as if it had been planned.

Here on our planet Earth we could learn from this star man
To care and to cherish, to do all that we can,
To plan and prepare for the final frontier,
So that future generations, need no longer know fear.

Carol Stocks

Forever's Edge

Another mission over shore leave arrives
Now spends his time by shores lapped by tides
Away from the city with his thoughts at last
The memories wash over tides that have passed.

He sails a ship that carries her name
Was it for her death that he was to blame
He stares at the sea but the waves are not seen
Kirk remembers a place where he has been.

To have bought this old schooner was he a fool
To ride a brown twig in a heaving pool
In a different time a different place
He gazed in pale light at her charming face.

He saw her in clothes that didn't suit her,
Her place was not there she belonged in the future
She strove for peace when war was needed
In matters of love Spock's warning was headed.

Sometimes he sees her in his nightmares,
She smiles at him and falls down dark stairs
To watch her die was it bad luck
That he could have scooped her away from the truck.

He stands on his schooner wood from a tree
Their love was fated not meant to be .

Michael Sadler

My TV Hero

I want you to guess in this little quiz
Who my number one TV hero is
Now I'll give you some clues to help you a bit
So persevere and don't just quit.

He's a tall, dark and handsome looking fellow
A starfleet commander who really suits yellow
He has a friend called Bones (who is actually a Doc)
And his second in command is a half-Vulcan called Spock.

He's Captain of a space ship called The Enterprise
Which travels at warp speed across future skies
And, when attacked, it creates an energy field
Which gives it a protective, invisible shield.

He battles with creatures from other worlds
But always wins as each plot unfurls
The Clingons are his number one threat
But they've never beaten my space hero yet.

His only weapon is a deadly laser gun
But being good and kind he sets it to stun
Because it's his brains and charm that wins the day
And he saves the Enterprise so they can all fly away.

Now his favourite saying is *Beam me up Scottie*
Then disappears - yes I know it sounds potty!
And with a blink of an eye, he's back on the ship
Ready for their next exciting trip.

So, have you guessed who my space hero is?
You know my name - but do you know his?
I gave you the clues but did they work
Yes, You knew all along - it's Captain James T Kirk.

Carolyn Brown

The Telephone Box

I always wear the same old clothes
I'm, always painted red
I stand here in the same old place, I never go to bed
People just pop in and out without consideration
All I ever seem to do is hear their conversation
Whatever they say it's safe with me, I pretend I never heard
Well even if I could speak I wouldn't tell a bird
When I'm out of order, people have only themselves to blame
They start to bang and kick me, everyone's the same
After they have finished they leave me in a mess
And say, 'you're always out of order, you're nothing but a pest.'
They leave me wrecked and shattered, standing in the rain
I feel so sad and lonely with my broken window pane
When people bang and kick me, whatever do they gain?
But still, I'm just the telephone box, it will always be the same.

The Late Charles William Frankham

Untitled

'Twas on Valentine this year,
On a dull and foggy day.
We, from the Midlands drove to Diva town.
To meet my family.
Amidst the happy chatter was
Shattered to find, that I was really blind.
Remembering that the week before
Whilst suffering from a mild migraine
And, hanging on to my daughter's arm,
Walked full tilt into a glass door *Wham*
In time, the blackness did fade to grey
Some vision did return but
Having an over all spotted effect
With only blackness on my left.
Now children dodge in front and below
And grown ups all as surprised as I
When we suddenly collide.
No abnormality from the brain scan
From one neurologist no lack of function
Except for some loss of sight. Lucky?
Cannot believe I had a stroke.
Continue swimming in the sea
Continue wood carving and bobbin lace
But No driving. Oh I do miss my car!
Now with a new baby grandaughter
Bethany by name - had hoped to be available
For minding her betimes, living
To far away for walking - and no buses.
When she visits can still see her
Little smiling face.

Theresa L Cox

The Articulated Attic-Agoraphobic

The rain down my neck; drip, drip
Whilst my wrought emotions; trip, trip,
What is beyond this canopy to heaven?
Or from my head; my sacred haven.
Memories of the murky past,
Coming back to me at last.
They were but yesterdays dreams;
Today they walk in mystical streams.
Where's that bubbling, babbling brook?
It's not inside this frowsty book!
Go outside and take a look,
You'll get there . . . by hook or crook.
Blank white paper reflects the light,
As I behold a sublime sight.
Rays from aloft enter my eyes,
And I gasp out a heartfelt sigh.
Bless the Lord for the strength he gives,
From up above, down to grubby dives.
In the gutter . . . look up to the stars,
And dream of chips and caviars.
No giddy-red, fast motorcars,
Spoiling cedarous, deodars
Where's the sense in writing a page,
When the country's in a rage?
Turn each other 'gainst t'others son,
And everyone will be anyone.
From my sanctuary the world I espy,
Though blind here within, I do but try
To feel the flight of the wingéd fly.
They're the same in Fareham and Fiji:
Need peace of mind, and to be free.

Charles McMullen

Moonstruck

I was struck by the moon,
    by its beauty
    its magical mystery
    and ancient history
I was struck by the moon,
    so permanent and watchful
    in the firmament so thoughtful looking
I was struck by the moon,
    not literally
        (which would've been sore)

Gordon Cameron

Why

Why is the world
Going down on its knees,
Why are we killing
The plants and the trees.
Why are the Rivers
Rising so high,
Why are there people
That starve and die.
Why can't we stop
The destruction and death,
Why do we seem to be
Wasting our breath.
Why don't we stand up
And fight for what's right,
Why don't we do something
To ease the world's plight.
Why don't we stop all this
Pollution and War
Why not let nature,
Even the score.
Why not repair
The Damage we've done,
Why not save the world
For your daughter or son.

R Mickleburgh

Reflections

I often lie and wonder why,
People near should ever die,
It seems so strange that to end their pain,
Leaves more for those who shall remain,
Our thoughts of death,
Are an unrest,
Not for ourselves,
But for those who are left.
We hope and wish that they can hear,
We like to think we feel them near,
It is normal to think of immediate pain,
But happy memories do remain.

Chlöe Butler

Silos to Rent

We are not concerned here with commoners' rights.
Come to Greenham, ignore the camps,
and grow mushrooms to withstand a nuclear attack.
You will boom with our heavily discounted rents.
Security will not be a problem with triple razor wire fencing,
and there will be power on tap for World War Three.
Does anyone have any questions?
Good. I cannot answer them.

Antony Rowland

Abbeyant Dissent

Seven laid
on sun kissed shores
golden dreams
dawn.
polynomial reams,
union spheres
harmony.

Now Mars prances
exclamation mark
did you see?
period
angels with lances,
wood on black,
the void . . .

Silver screen
not for your eyes,
have you heard?
lament.
aperture sieves
descending thieves
lament.

Highway ride,
(twelve bandits hide)
bullets fly,
disdain.
Here arrogance rules
where angels lie,
abyss.

Fru Constantine

Dark Shadows

Moon bright, Teeth glinting,
Scarlett dribbling over lips,
Drink my soul again.

Cardinal Cox

Moon Landing

Couldn't they
 have left the stars alone?
  traces
   across
    the screen
     of night -
Absent
 like faces
  only remembered -
Because
 they once disturbed.

Robert Pim

The Human Race

Strange little alien
from outer space.
Funny shaped head,
little green face.
One little eye in
the middle of his brow,
He can't speak our language,
he doesn't know how.
What is he doing here,
this visitor from space?
He's here to investigate
the human race.
He looks at us with interest,
amazement in his eye.
He sees that we're all different,
but he doesn't know why.
Some rather large,
others very small.
Some quite slim,
some with no shape at all!
He looks at our food -
mountains of chips!
He sees people smoking,
cigarettes between their lips,
There's a look of amazement
on his little green face
What will he make
of the human race?

Mavis Fox

UFO

Oh strange unidentified flying object
Known as a UFO
On your mysterious journey
Through the night you go
Are you from some distant star?
Desiring to *Shake a hand*
Or a radio - controlled *spy ship*
From some ill-intentioned foreign land?
Your *wild erratic movements*
Mere man cannot explain:
Can you see me, watching you
Through my window - pane?
Do you patrol our hemisphere
To save us from destruction?
Or *Just interested* in our feats,
Of invention and construction?
Maybe, you are *Devil Powered*
Filled with only hate?
Or *Modernly transported angels*
Keen to learn our fate?
Whatever you are, probably,
I shall never know?
As shedding blue and orange sparks
As quickly as you came - you go!

Gaenor Spratley

Heroes All

Doctor Who went to the Zoo,
To visit talking cockatoo.

How absurd this cocky bird,
Only spoke in old Hindu.

If that cock had been a gannet,
It would have gulped, *Forbidden Planet*

Only Spock with his big ears,
Heard the news of Star War fears.

Did strife or bit close to Heaven,
Traversed by the bold Blake's Seven?

The peacemaker was pretty Lottie,
Who smiled and said, 'Beam me up Scottie.'

Captain Kirk received a rocket
For smuggling Lithium in his pocket.

ET began to change his sex
And to dance home with black Daleks.

In studio five, crusading cape
Had muddled up the video tape.

Avoid the poison berries Logan,
And help promote a poet Vogan.

Peter N Lawrence

The Dark Planets

Many millions of light years away
We might get to know, someday
If there's life on the planets so dark
And if on them man can make his mark.

UFO's have come down to earth, some say
To take back samples of earth and clay
For analysing in another place
Is there a Super Human Race?

Despite all that man has done
He can't control the rain or sun
Maybe one day we will see why
Man can't control the unquiet sky.

Maria Young

The End of the World

The light of the world has gone out,
Darkness covers the land
The sea cries a tear of ash on an empty shore
No waves rush upon the beach the world lies dead,
Where once man walked
For time has ended for man he is no more
His world lies dead and darkness covers the land
Like night without end
Only the wind remains
such a cruel wind that
Once scattered the flower petals around
With seeds of mankind
But now they have all gone
And lonely the wind cries in an endless night.

Henry M F Djuritscher

Tomorrow

There is more to space than we think;
much more. Much more.
Travel beyond the furthest star
and you'll find it's an open door
to Infinity beyond.

Fantasy tries to describe
the world we will one day see.
Beyond the limitless space
of Tomorrow there yet will be
worlds to settle, to people;
to learn from mistakes of our own;
worlds where high adventure
and the seeds of love will be sown.

We cannot even envisage
try as we may in our mind
to think of the life that will flourish
and the joy our race will find.

It is all there - waiting -
while the stars in their courses sing
their shining song of Tomorrow
and the wonders space will bring.

Diana Morcom

Beings From Space

You rub your eyes, think it's a dream
But is that a spaceship that you have just seen
a robot is coming through the door
behind it a floating figure, followed by several more
You stand there staring, eyes open wide
they extend the hand of friendship, and welcome you inside
they are a very caring people, a very loving race
and they leave you feeling sad as they go back into space
one day they might return when all wars on earth cease
and people of this world of ours learn to live in peace.

Patricia Maynard

Moon Man

Look out kids, here comes the moon man
Gleaming in silver and grey,
Those eyes that are lighting like beacons
Are they meaning to steal you away?

Hurry kids down to the clearing
To the craft there of silvery grey,
Settled down deep in the forest,
Looks like it's aiming to stay.

Whoops kids, engines are churning.
Lifting it into the sky
Where are the kids who were hiding
Vanished, without a goodbye.

Ann Rutherford

Concealed Deepness

Inside this empty sphere the riddle of it all,
Lightness, darkness, smallness, tall,
Who has the answer, the question is I am,
I look up at history, I see it twinkle bright,
Or is it just a phantom shell, the past of the night.
Burning intense, cooling cold
A new born child getting old,
Sing a song, make a noise
Play with an infinity of toys,
Who says there is no reason,
The reason is why.

Leslie Heaps

Supper

Peeking out on a cold Winter's night
She wonders at the pale moonlight
Glowing through sapphired skies
And watched by telescopic eyes.

Where little newborn stars rest
Protected by the honeycombed breast
Waiting for the explosive rides
Through milky ways and ocean tides.

The Big Dipper, the Bear and Aries
All covet the nocturnal fairies
Sprinkling golden dust at dusk
- Supper for the shimmering cusp.

But far beyond the Cosmos, activities
Defying surely spacial gravity's
Exists a Universe of mystifying things
Like Aliens, Starships and solar rings.

And when she shuts her sleepy eyes,
Will she dream of the Enterprise?
Flying through a starry constellation
- A fuelling stop for the child's imagination

Gay Sorah

Heavenly Courtship

I read of spaceships - Lord what twist
of verbal plunder, what grimace of thought
squeals in these common syllables, what ache
in the worn mind groans for the groaning's sake,
how zealously we chase the prey we sought,
the soaring bird, the love of loving missed.

We sailed, oh yes, we sailed, we bumped the stars,
figged at the moon battered the bars of rain,
fought in a frenzy, netted in the sheets
of clouds square-rigged, tumbled on the seats
annexed by wonder, goggled at the chain
dripping with ice and shining red like Mars.

And then we crashed! The splinters pierced our limbs
we cried in anguish, spat out broken teeth,
caught at our breath, arranged our broken bones
and filled our pockets with curses and little moans.
The sky's still there but we are underneath,
crawling in pain on the planet's poisoned rims.

John Atkins

Aliens Star Trek

Where do they come from
And where do they go
How do they get her
I'd like to know.

Are they illusions
Or real solid things
And how can they fly
If they haven't got wings.

How are they powered
Does nobody know
Without any motors
How far can they go.

They do not have features,
That we can define
And their legs are transparent
For most of the time.

If they haven't got features
Then how can they breathe
So why wear a spacesuit
There's really no need.

Now some people claim
To have travelled inside
Which lead's me to think
I've been took for a ride.

S J Clarke

Star Wars

They waged war with their space guns and their fierce laser rays
For science had furnished their horrid displays,
Which made those old wars of the Grecian gods
Appear like a battle of children with rods.
Foes were melted like ice in a high blazing fire
Or trampled to death like a slug in the mire,
Are these then the scenes predicted for Man
No glimpses of Mercy or Peace could we scan.
What ills do these pictures of carnage portend
What are the lessons and where will it end,
Where men carry to Space every weapon malign
Assuming that such is the Cosmic design.
Are they blind to the pleas for the blessings of Peace
Or the Joys that true Kinship must ever release,
Shall we who have managed this Earth to deface
Bear all our perversions afar into Space.
Or is there a way where transgressions lie dead
Where men to true Freedom and Safety are led,
Can voices from Heaven show us the way
Far better than that which we Earthlings display.
Are there Masters ascended who seek to intrude
To show us the pathway to true Brotherhood.

O come foolish Man seek no such advice
Be not as the bat or as feeble as mice,
For right here on Earth is the Remedy found
Where the Themes of Redemption and Glory abound.

Tom Burns

Sentimental Journey into Space

It doesn't seem very long to me,
Since wireless was the rage,
We'd gather round, when school was done
To tune in whatever our age.

I think my first radio Sci-Fi treat,
Was *Journey into Space*, with
Bill Kerr and David Jacobs' tones,
We really thought them *Ace*.

Then along came mass TV oh
Didn't we enjoy the time,
Spent with the Quatermass Experiment
Covering all with root or slime.

We then had Star Trekkies taking off,
With Captain Kirk and Spock,
To *Beam us up* and *Boldly Go*,
Looking for Klingons or even Doc.

Let's not forget our Doctor Who,
Blakes 7 and Star Wars pending,
Forbidden Planet, Planet Apes,
And special effects unending.

And oh, the thrill of Flash Gordon's smile,
I'd almost quite forgotten,
Sitting in the back row stalls,
Frightened something rotten.

Is my memory playing tricks on me,
For when Sci-Fi first began, it seems,
We Earthlings laughed our fear away,
And kept to the bright side of our dreams.

L M Green

Man From Mars

What's that strange light
Zooming above me?
Can't be a plane - what can it be!
It's landing before my very eyes.
Where is it from - could it be Paradise?
A very tall figure emerging from this thing -
Can't see it's eyes, it walks with a swing.
It seems to beckon me towards it's ship.
I move back in fear, I almost slip.
With a nod of its head, and a pointed finger.
Seems instead, not wanting to linger.
Climbs aboard this peculiar thing -
I almost felt I wanted to sing.
As it soars away toward the stars,
I sigh with relief, could it have come from Mars,
I shall never forget that unusual sight.
That left me speechless through the night.
No one else saw it - so it seems.
Perhaps it was another of my bad dreams!

W M Jeffery

Time Dilitantation oh! Chére Amie in Old Santiago

(Log Entry by Col Gene Pool subordinate to Capt T Cric)

Kirch to Earth requesting a small advance in pay
when I return by earthy count I'll be ten thou' today.

Earth here calling up to Captain Iago Kirch
boldly gone somewhere out there on pioneering work

Far into the unknown beyond the outer rime
Odysseys conjectural in distance and in time

the source here knows your origin which is here on earth
we are waiting for an answer . . . state your rank
and number, also date of birth.
Don't give me all that red tape, send it all to hell
pile up my back wages (and the small advance as well!)

We must have this information (so the speaker drones)
how else can we differentiate, we are yourselves . . .
. . . your clones
androgynous replication has done away with sex
the orders all been changed around,
while you were out on trecks
bring in that ship this minute, and settle up your due
school fees and rates and tax compound are debited to you.

My last will and my testament to you my latter Kirch
are, I've many things to see about so I'm going back to work

and within a fortnight (ten thousand years to you)
I'll be back with all these ladies, meanwhile you know
what you can . . .

B Charles

Fiction Into Fact

They seek them here,
They seek them there,
They gaze up in the sky,
At times I really do despair
And ask the reason why
That Captain Kirk and Klingons
Make such visual impact,
And where Dr Who's opinion
Is an academic fact.

If there really are such aliens
Living happily in Mars,
With lots of television screens
Showing life among the stars,
Then we've become in turn to them,
The story of the human men.
Confirming fiction then as fact
(How would our scientists react.)

So, when next you hire a video
Of Science Fiction at its best,
Just give a seconds thinking
As you watch the worlds conquest,
That this is a rehearsal
For the days that are to come,
When we use our own equipment
And fly safely past the Sun.

Anne Dunseath

Silence!

The Moon has no sound,
No life,
No undergrowth dense,
No thud or pound,
Not even a sound.

Imagine it there,
The Moon and no light,
Just dark black sky
Empty and bare,
Imagine it there,
Wouldn't you care?

The Moon has no sound,
No undergrowth dense,
No thud or pound,

No not even a sound . . . !

Amy Rodulfo

Lone Flyer

Deep in the world's external night
my spacecraft thunders by.
Where colours glow in eerie light
and where no wind can sigh.

Somewhere a rock in speedy mass
will cause my craft to stray.
And stars' quick gleam is where I pass
and where there is no day.

But soon my missions' end is nigh
I see the earthlight dear.
Re-entry over, down I fly
My heaven is surely here.

Maureen Warner

Life

Not yet a Being
In spiritual state
The Embryo of Life
Forged through cosmic rays.

Changes of climate it experienced
On worlds yet to be discovered
Nearing Earth its destination
It heard the cries and felt the pain
An existence they called Civilisation

In a telepathic call
Great Spirit of us all
Help me when I am born
To make a good and loving race.

Joyce W Hamlett

Vanishing Dog

The aliens came to Earth one day,
And transported my best friend away!
They said, 'We come from the planet Zog.
'We want to interview your dog!'
The saucer in the sky flew higher
And was lit like a bright metallic fire.
I missed my friend for five whole days
With his wagging tail and funny ways.
On his return, complete with bone
He said, 'I've just come back from the Twilight Zone!'
'What did you do there?' I said to him.
'Have you noticed nothing,' he replied with a grin.
'You look your old self to me
Come on I'll get you your favourite tea.'
I came back with your usual dish of meat,
But you were sat on the corner seat,
Talking down our telephone,
Presumably to the Twilight Zone!

Dee Chapman

The Meteor

A fragment of some star perhaps,
The meteor drifts thro' seas of night,
Beholding all the awesome scenes
Of stars and planets in their flight:

Past Mars, its reddish atmosphere
Of dust, from deserts wild and flat;
Canals of emptiness give life
To lifeless forms of this and that.

Past cunning Venus, beauty hid
Beneath a covering cloak of cloud;
See Saturn slowly make his way
Sedately, dignified and proud.

Now past the planet Earth so green;
The sun shines on her beauteous face,
But on and on the meteor sails,
E'en to the very shores of space.

Mary Hayworth

Missing you

Let's face the fact
That we need some space
To remain intact

But

it's

l
o
n
e
l
y

out

i
n

e
c
a
p
s

Julie Humphries

Kirk County

Space: the final frontier
swarming with eager thespians
of wood in sixties costume
Power-mad, intelligent, and
peace-mongering, they trek
a sex-life, seemingly minus genitalia
it's all in the mind
or on the bridge

Pride and shame in
homosapiens, inspired by
misanthropes and helpless
class *M* planets, the
gamut of emotion flows
while we eat our tea
in TV astonishment
Shields down and stunned
'These co-ordinations on my mark . . . '

Enterprising excursions speed -
streaking light-blurred in
winking silence, beamed
aboard the diplomatic mobile
enclave, assumed in orbit,
if Scotty can keep it there
a few more hours; when all
we have are minutes and
seconds logged away in space . . .

Alex Oliver

Fools and Angels

In our very act of conversation
There is a secrecy,
Words are no trouble for us
And looks come easily.
Subjects weave and intertwine
And inner worlds rise and fall
With our breath.

Between us
Eternal present flows,
You are all
I have ever known:
    lace and crystal
    pearls and music
    scenes from a thousand paintings.

I can say I love you
And we know it has always been true.

I demand nothing from you
Yet have everything,
I walk away
Knowing you will always be with me.

By thought
We lose all we once held on to,
Through feeling
All we have is real.

Mine is the world of fools and angels
There you are my lover and my friend.

Graham Guest

Attack of the Planets

Silent tension in the black
Deep of the Galaxy awaiting attack,
Stars all hide and shade their light
Are there to watch but not in sight.
Sun is sleeping as it pulses red
And the moon is rising from its floating bed,
The Universe lined with an army of planets
Forming two barricades, strong as a magnet.
Each crater contained filled full ammunition
Pride is important, if not loss of position,
Like an itch in the sky, anxiety breaks
Enduring on, the Black Holes' invisible lake.
The moments anticipation ceases to trigger
Attack of the Planets, in full rage of vigour,
Mars is first to fire its force
But callous actions cloud remorse.
Like a spiralling merry-go-round they coax to crash
Whilst Mercury teases, too small to lash,
Sparks of moon dust fly through the dark
Saturn battles bravely but its weapons are stark.
Uranus struggles in silence with Neptune
As Pluto darts like a fire fly, but all too soon,
For Venus has shed it's white and now orbits in black
Not even Earth survived this attack.
The great sphere of Jupiter roars loud to end
Battle of the Planets, where no one body defends
As the shooting star of life fades as it descends.

Lindsay Sayers

Avon Calling

I wish I could be in Blake's Seven
But alas it's not on anymore,
I had a strong love for Avon
That filled me to the pore.

I'd love to tour the stars with him
But I guess it's just too late.
He'd be my number seven
And I his number eight.

He was so vibrant on the box
And used to entertain us.
We could be Mars and Venus
But I'd call a halt on Uranus.

Linda M Windsor

My Days With the Star Trek Mob

When Jimbo said to Scotty
'Beam me up old man,'
he pressed his little button
and he was gone wam bam.

I love to watch Jim Kirk
and Spock he is the best
with Doc McCoy and Scotty
and all the bloomin' rest.

I watch them on the TV
and video as well
I love to see Jim Kirk
I think he's really swell.

I'd press all the buttons
to beam me down and up
I'd play with weird chess games
then I would dress up,

In out of date old clothes
and I'd have Spocky's ears
I'd sit upon the bridge
for years and years and years.

Jim, he is the captain
and I would be his mate
with Doc McCoy
I'd really like a date.

Tracie Anne McDonald

Star Date Log Enterprise to Intrepid Time - Twelve . . . Two . . . Nine

O' star date time, twelve, two, nine
high low flying cloud
And logic on the line
on an impulse, forward thrust
with Scotty, stabilising the warp speed climb.

Capt' Kirk had closed the bridge
had Dr Bone's, dem bones, dem bones, dem bones
Mr Spock, Mr Chechov and us, the only survivors
on the Enterprise space shuttle probe.

And out into the Entry Zone
Capt' Kirk gave clear his orders
Lt Uhura gave tele channel audio test clear
at the order from the bridge
'Examine the reproductive, impact, cromosones.'

'It's on the telecom,' whispered Lt Uhura,
'energise and beam the lifeless life aboard.'
Mr Scott, heightened the communication shield
Pulsed, and pulled the amoeba at the life support cord.

'We are in their boundary layer,' gasped Mr Spock.
Muttered, 'Others would not have survived.'
The logic of the illogical, stand by, Logarithms
Ment, space, all space, no space, with no space to hide.

We had found, at the centre of the Universe, an amoeba
Mr Sulu threw up the viewing screen
'What is it?' asked Dr McCoy.
'It's life, lifeless life,' answered Jim.
'It's Death and Life at the centre of Life's Universe.'
'It's like all things that have and are, Death and Life.'
And all things that have, are, and been, and our *being.*

R J Collins

The Rise and Fall of Mr Spock and Scotty!

Flying through space at top warp speed.
Mr Spock says, 'Scotty take heed!
You are travelling at one thousand miles a minute,
You should know you're way over the limit!'
Scotty says, 'Well it won't take as long
To reach the empire of the dreaded Clingon!'

'At last we're here, anyone see a ship?'
Then on the horizon appeared a blip.
Mr Spock said, 'Man the lasers
And while you're at it man the phasers!'

The ship slowed down and finally came to a stop!
'Ooops!' said Scotty and the ship started to drop!
'Abandon ship!' Mr Spock called.
'It's all Scotty's fault that we stalled!'

Everyone jumped out . . .

Silence . . .

Then Scotty said, trying to be funny,
'Oh well Spock, no more money
From doing that film they call *Star Trek.*'
'Well think yourself lucky Scotty that we escaped
from the space wreck!'

David Petra (12)

Where no Man Has Gone

Eidolons of man's desire,
They rend the veils of stars and time,
Seeking beyond those spheres of fire,
The strength of his evolving climb.

Time and space, their rims unknown
To us of mortal finite years,
So imaginations seeds are sown
To quell the rise of futile tears.

Born from mind, the travellers go,
Their silver ships on plumes of fire,
Beyond the gates we all do know,
Star to star, we too aspire.

With Kirk and Spock, McCoy and Scott,
We trace the lanes of velvet night,
From diamond dwarf to giant hot,
The stars in splendour shed their light.

Beacons to emergent dreams,
They draw, as moths to a flame,
Calling first, imagined themes,
Then man himself to play the game.

Peter Rowe

The Final Frontier

Captain Kirk stood on the bridge,
On this particular day.
He was searching all of space for Klingons,
To blow them all away.

He asked first officer Spock,
If he had any idea where they were.
Give me an answer if you will.
Everything that he was ever asked,
Spock just said illogical.

He made the Enterprise go up to Warp Factor three,
Sat on his chair and had a cup of tea.
Scottie came over the intercom,
In his Yankee-Scottish tones,
'I canna hold her Jim.'
Jim said, 'Oh I've got a headache, fetch me Bones.'

Leslie Heaps

2001 - the Return

They came as before
Suddenly, unseen and unheard
No need this time to land
Or to seed the good earth
With a cool, black obelisk.

Instead they
Circled above
Looked down
Tapped into
Our lives.

It took
Two minutes
An average
Length for
Television ads.

And what passed for sadness
Registered a fleeting moment
Before they were gone again
Making a mental note to return -
When we had grown up.

Richard Stewart

The Healing of Worlds

Journey, journey, through the space,
The young star riders setting the pace,

Searching the heavens feeling the force,
Love honesty and freedom the hopeful course,

Starfleets to sail the wondrous height,
Asteroids with burning trails of light,

Commanders feeding the thirst for knowledge,
Radio waves calling, acknowledge,

For ever to see the silver Christmas display,
Orbiting worlds around the galaxy to play,

Each star world to make their demands,
Reaching for the healing of universal hands.

Nick Steel

It Like Obliterates

From beyond a thing.
So hidden and unseen.
It like obliterates.
And deforms it.
Into multicultural and
Often obscure shapes.
Strong are these.
Modern urban tendencies.
So lax and tame.
Are the very weak.
Several weeks can.
Go fast if
You let them pass.
You by like the wind.
That savage wind.
That blows its strong eddy.
What does it blow.
Like that way for.
Is it nature's way.
Saying all will go on.
And on 'til new things arrive.
What will the new things be?
And what will they be like?

Richard Clewlow

The Unenterprising Woman!

I ponder the possibilities and ask? Could I be out there in space.
To Captain the Enterprise in place of good old Kirk,
A woman at the helm, why not? I'm not only fair of face,
But stalwart, keen, fit for all jobs I'll not shirk.
What of *Bones* with his magic touch?
A lady, not Jim, well that could be just too much!
Poor old *Scottie* and all his beaming folk up quick,
To hear his *mistresses* voice, might not do the trick!
Poor Spock with his alien ears, and oh! so puzzled brow,
Will it be logical to have a lady show *him*, her know-how?
Then the ship, vast city in the sky, alert and ready for her word,
Changing the name to *Excalibur*, wasn't that Arthur's sword?
But change we must accept, be bold and voyage afar,
On this new ship's magical exploits to another distant star.
If at the helm a woman plots each new unchartered course,
Confronting aliens less friendly then, battle shields ready of course!
Today there is no equality or sex discrimination we hear,
So forward starship *Excalibur* and cross yet this new frontier!

Joyce M Hefti-Whitney

Stormy Trek

The sun diminishes, brightness dulls
Enterprise accelerates, gravity pulls
Past Earth, interstellar space
Observe the scanner, heed the pace.

The sun resembles yet another star
Since blast off, we've come so far
The sensor data screens its waves
Pulsating spectrums of coloured rays.

At the command chair, sits Captain Kirk
Always vigilant, not one to shirk
With Bones and Scotty, some of his crew
On the bridge sits the navigator Sulu.

Enterprise glides smoothly on coarse
Accurate perception from alien force
At the rear view, a turquoise sphere
Could that be Saturn, we're orbiting near.

Aura skies bathed in orange velvet
A pock marked moon, circles a planet
Illuminating a myriad of stars
As McCoy utters, one might be Mars.

Computer signals cease to function
Which caused a lot of anxious tension
It's an antimatter storm, shouts Spock
See the orbiting clouds, we'll dock.

The mission continues, Kirk commanded
As it won't be long before we've landed
And once we reach the satellite
The crew of Enterprise, will be alright.

Shirley Sperry

Doctor Who

Who is Doctor Who?
Where does he live?
Does he have a mum?
That's the questions I would give
He never seems to age,
Fighting monsters single handed,
Never getting in a violent rage,
On the many planets he has landed,
I think he should write a book,
On how he survived all his disasters,
It might give us some advice
On how to look after our world
Forever after.

C Oliver

Football on the Moon

There's a football match on the moon;
The stadium they hope to fill.
The seats have been fastened to the ground,
And they've taken their gravity pill.

Humans are very clever
To have reached the moon at all,
But one thing they've completely forgotten:
To gravitise the ball.

The players are running and leaping,
But, however hard they try,
They cannot kick that moonstruck ball,
Which twists and turns in the sky.

The audience are in hysterics:
It's upsetting their gravity pill;
They jump and shout and fling about
But they just cannot keep still.

Legs are mixed with arms:
They clutch at somebody's thigh.
They are upside down or sideways on,
As the ball goes sailing by.

At last they abandon the strife;
All hopes of winning have flown.
And there is the ball underneath the net;
It has got there on its own.

Muriel P Knight

The Shore of Infinity

Motionless
In the centre of the open field,
Head craning backwards
Gazing at the distant stars.
Pinpricks of icy light pierce inky blackness
Like minute chinks in a celestial curtain
Shielding us from the immensity of space,
The infinity of the universe.

I am dwarfed, engulfed under that aloof, frosty gaze,
Become invisible, insignificant in the vastness above.
Tiny, a grain of sand drifting along the shore of infinity,
Buffeted, whirled and tossed upon the current of life.

Are others out there too?
Across unimaginable distances,
Light years away across the void.
Do they too look up from their alien planet
Circling an unknown sun?
Do they too gaze at the stars above
Wondering, awed?
Maybe they live in paradise,
Maybe they live in hell,
Most likely they live in a little of each,
Just like us
But impossible, impassable aeons away
Across the boundless gulf,
Circling an unknown star,
Not even visible from earth.

Kiran Gayle Harvey

Blake's Seven Lament

Tears fell like rain that time,
Words wouldn't sound good or rhyme,
As if blazing fire fell from the sky,
Or the universe quickly did die.

Wrapped in a science-fiction dream,
We gave forth an agonised scream,
Life as we knew it suspended,
At the way Blake's Seven ended.

Robert Parker-Munn

Curried Egg

An egg was laid, a handsome young fella
his proud parents names were Sam an' Ella!
Alas, a delicate child couldn't play out at all
his parents had to wrap him up in warm cotton wool.
As he grew older, he wanted to play and join in
his folks tried to warn him his shell was especially thin.
No climbing up trees or walking along a wall
a child that does that will undoubtedly fall.
He thought he knew best he didn't really care,
he intended to have some fun when his parents weren't there.
He climbed up the wall and sat down on the top
he started to sway and then began to flop.
He hurtled to the ground and cracked open his head
his insides spilt out and he laid there quite dead.
The king's men were passing such gallant young folk
but they couldn't stop him from spilling his yolk.
His parents came back they were in such a state
they couldn't do anything to alter their son's fate.
Humpty Dumpty was his name you've probably heard the rhyme
young children are told it, by their parents all the time.
You'll probably not know a large cat sitting near
began to hiss and spit filling everyone with fear.
The people moved back, the cat's tail gave a flick
she neared the shattered body and quickly began to lick.
Before anyone could stop her, she finished the yolk and white
nobody dared to approach her in case she should scratch or bite.
The cat died that day she was in too much of a hurry
to dismiss all the advice given by Mrs Edwina Currie.
You see you shouldn't eat eggs that haven't been cooked
that is one piece of advice the cat had overlooked.
Humpty Dumpty had salmonella, that's food poisoning you know
if you get an upset tummy to the doctor's you must go.
And if you get better, you'll have learnt the hard way,
that eating uncooked eggs just isn't safe today!

Gill Plumb

Haytor Heaven

Beneath the Great Tor's billowing shadow
My mind wanders lonely as a cloud
Gentle the breezes that stir my senses
My heart swells at the site of her

Amber eyes glint dark and wary
My footsteps tread the granite tramway
She trots still watchful at my countenance
If I stop and eat she will undoubtedly stay

Tiny houses scatter the valley like droplets
Eyes stretch to where land meets the ocean
And Bovey nestles like a broody peahen
At the gates to heaven's own enchanted land

The vixen retreats with watchful glances
Home to her bundles of new life
I turn my thoughts to the journey onward
And see a man poised to render this hour his own

The kit, the cameras, the earthy hues
Sanguine tourists pass in a heady blur
To capture some of Dartmoor's more mystical mood
Gentle giant and keeper of some other folks' souls

I court the black tarmac ribbon homeward
Stepping down from swollen sward
My vision drunk from too much beauty
An illicit promise of all our tomorrows

Isabella Shaw

The Rocking Chair

The rhythmic creak of a rocking chair
A mind flits back through all the years,
Not for it the fading monochrome photograph
But a cacophony of moving images.
Memories brought to life each night
Adding interest and a little joy,
To one who's life was spent in the grime
And dust amongst the whirling machines
on the factor floor.

How the advent of colour brought a
New depth and meaning;
Strangers became as friends,
Dispelling the greys and whites,
Allowing a dazzling insight of what could be,
If only.
Time has passed
A mind flits back,
A meaningless screen flickers nearby
The rhythmic creak of the rocking chair.

Robin Shea

Reaching Out

In tenderness reaching out,
finding hard to speak it
Courage lacking I hide in print
Trouble is, now said, I'm missing
Strength to meet
the stranger
Uncomfortable, hesitating and clumsy
could I be
searching for right to say
with so much unsaid.

Ron Constant

The Water Table

Beside the pond, acquaintance
And I sat,
A table where swifts and martins
Collect and feast at.
A feast for the eye were these
Morsels,
Sharpness of form slicing the air,
Watching precision on the wing
Without care.
Tilting and skimming their bodies,
So close to the pond,
With a curve of suddenness,
Regaining height,
Amazement and pure delight
We both respond.
To observe one of these birds,
A keen eye is well endowed,
For the black silhouette, lost
Within the crowd.
A mixture of black, white, blue
Is the arena of view.

Ron David Zussner

My Lifeline

Choking; choking, drowning in my sea of sputum
Thick black tar of execution
Death bed cries, fear multiplies
In a vortex of pollution.
I inhaled comfort, and in so doing
Allowed euphoric smoke, to cloak my naive
Mind to ruin.

Gasping; gasping, burning lungs are fighting
Stop this frightening rasp - the file of their escape.
Passive sharing, passive caring.
Not hooked onto this pleasure?
I will give you my full measure
Of precious nicotine.

Come one, come all
My voice is weak
I cannot call this message loud
I strive to survive the oncoming end
I ask you my friend, to let them know
How I suffered for acceptance
It is a miserable way to go.

Delyse Harrison

Christmas: Disparates Assembled

Lagan of the rich man's marriages
have that one link, tentacular.
They're stuck for days together,
near strangers to each other.

Asked-in guests can't cloak the awkwardness.
It's cramped and hot. The current wife's
called for the smaller house.
Such hard work unless . . .

Massed loaded silver kickshaw dishes
capsize the little table.
Festoons and fronded tinsel stir
in overheated air,

moved by survivors' talk: for only breath's expired.
The hovercraft! We ground that out of business.
Do you know what the costs are,
state schools in Westminster?

Sunk treasure's sunk and won't be shared.
Depleted, now, the nut hoard:
emerging silver spaces image
shining, swag.

P S Joll

Moon Walking

Television science fiction has never appealed to me.
Life is stranger than any fiction, as far as eye can see.
The only series I recall was all about the moon.
They put men there by rocket, return trip by balloon.
They did it fairly well, the launch was quite exciting.
On the moon they slow-motion bounced, shot in grainy lighting.
To make them seem a long way off, more authentic, scientific,
They spoke in muffled voices, very croaky, laryngitic.
Most of the cast were on the earth, and almost all were men.
There were no glamorous girl scientists, but then,
There were no creatures either, benign or just plain nasty.
They made the moon a dull old place, that is, if you ask me.

She really is more exciting, just take a walk at night.
If you go East, she'll follow on the right.
If you walk North, then you'll find,
She'll follow you, just close behind.
If you stop, then so will she.
No matter what you do, her luminous eye will see.
In the television series, they brought some moon rock home,
Boring, shapeless, like a piece of buried bone.
What nonsense. I know she's not made of cheese,
(Any more than she sent her man down for a wheeze),
But smooth and silvery, more like ice.
You see her in the morning sky, just a melting slice.
She can dissolve quite slowly in the darkest of the nights,
And glass-brittle, break into a thousand glowing lights.

She is a beautiful presence, a celestial mystery.
Trying to explain her is pure moonshine, lunacy.

Ronald King

Enemy Mine

On a planet cold, and desolation
His space ship crashed beyond repair
Above in the sky alive with electric flame
Fighters battering out with exact aim,
Finding to eat what he can
Though he heard the sound of another man
Being alone like Man Friday.
From out of hiding came another being
Could not believe what he was seeing,
He was like Morph and spoke double dutch
They came friends and liked one another so much.
They taught each other their native tongue
On a cold snowy day
Another alien being conceived on the planet Souse
Man Friday promised on its death bed.
To befriend it as the alien being in its eyes tears shed
To bring it up as its own.
As to man death it would be prone
Just like a child it became
Playing and enjoyed childhood games,
He was kidnapped and to be put into slavery.
He was rescued by Man Friday
Never again would they part,
Man Friday had love in his heart
Just like a father with a son
Until the end of time Enemy Mine.

M Burridge

Lovers United by Death in City of Hatred

News of love travels fast
Microphone echoes and bold print
Vague scenes, seen obscure.

News of love travels slow
Coaxing peace via pain
Report tragedy, encourage society.

News of love a refugee
Encumbered arms, mortally perfumed
Stretched stiff and paraded asunder.

News of love a martyr
Butchered on a day
And dead from sight.

Amish Chauhan

Thoughts and Queries (Extract)

Thought - Theoretically *insane* is the opposite of being *out of sane* i.e., out of sanity and therefore not of a fine mental state. So if out sane is mental then insane is not mental and is therefore sane. So when we say someone is insane we actually mean that they are of a perfect mental state, so insane is a complement. The correct wording to use would be *out-sane* or even *un-sane.*

Query - If the Bogeyman lives in the dark then wouldn't he be a bit of a hazard? That is, forever bumping into things or tripping over things or knocking things off tables etc. Well this certainly explains the phrase 'Things going bump in the night.'

Thought - When people say, 'It happens to the best of us.' It doesn't. This is simply because *they* are better than us so won't let whatever *it* is affect them. If they did however they couldn't be classed as better, they could only be ranked as equal, so why can't people stop quoting this phrase wrongly and instead say something to the effect of 'it happens to the equals of us'?

Query - If the right hand is so called because we write with it why is it still called the right hand for left handed people who write with their left hand? Strange!

Thought - If the Three Wise Men were so wise, why did they bring the baby Jesus such useless gifts as gold, frankincense and myrrh? Surely they'd realise that a rattle, a dummy and some nappies would be of more use to him.

S Taylor (17)

Pictures Telling Stories

Art is a form of language
Pictures from ones mind
Telling people stories
They normally could not find.

Putting brush to canvas
Relating to what they see
It's another way of writing
I think you will agree.

Pictures telling stories
Of present and of past
Art showing peoples patience
Takes time can't be completed fast.

Showing peoples harmony
In the world in which they live
Expressing feelings not shown in books
Pleasure to the eyes it gives.

Some Artists are said to be ingenious
Others thought to be insane
As they put their brush to canvas
They've a message to convey.

Using every detail possible
Their story it is told
Some believe in arts message so deeply
They emboss its frame in gold.

Stephen T Maslen

Venus

Alone and serene in the Western sky,
None can reach her, none may try,
A diamond set in indigo,
The long years pass her by.

Like Icarus, she flies too near the Sun,
Her oceans boil and metals run.
A heavenly ship, with sails unfurled?
No,
Just another hostile world.

John Tirebuck

Star Trek

I'm a trekky there's no doubt about it,
I want to shout it to the world
and let my feelings ring out about me.

Who said they are past it and ageing too,
they are showing the reruns on Channel 4 too.
Bones and Spock and Chekov too,
are some of the bestest crew.

Captain Slog, I said who.
I never did find that member of the crew.
Captain Kirk, now you are talking.
What a fine figure of a man, to go moon walking.

The trouble with Tribbles, is, they bounce off
your head. You find them in the cupboard and
under your bed.
They have taken over the Enterprise, in every
form, you will even find them in the ship's hold.
Spock would say, in all this commotion.
It just isn't logical sir, without emotion.

Petrina G Tatnall

Alternatives

Happy or sad,
Good or bad,
Laugh or cry,
Out spoken or shy.

Quiet or loud,
Timid or proud,
Real or pretend,
Enemy or friend.

Poor or wealthy,
Sick or healthy,
Old or new,
Talk or argue.

Heartbroken or glad,
Content or mad,
Smiles or tears,
Shouts or cheers.

Reserved or wild,
Adult or child,
Stupid or clever,
Perhaps or never.

Tough or weak,
Scruffy or chic,
Feeble or strong,
Right or wrong.

Pompous or caring,
Mean or sharing,
Blind or observing,
Rich or deserving.

Sarah Maycock

Anderson's Astronauts

5, 4, 3, 2, 1, Thunderbirds are Go
So Gerry Anderson begins,
The countdown to another show
International Rescue always wins.

Those famous numbers refer of course
Not only to the blast
Off, but the craft, the very source
Of success which came fast.

Jeff Tracy and his fearless boys
Are ever at the ready
To charge down any evil ploys
So cool and smart and steady.

Alan, Virgil, Scott and John
Are heroes not puppet toys,
Whose rocket flames and lights have shone
Like the faces of watching boys.

Hackenbacker also known as *Brains*
For most the star, the cream,
Genius with trains and boats and planes,
Scientist of the team.

Tracey Island's home to all these *friends*,
Their dream isle in the sun,
Which to many weekly sends
A whoosh of sci-fi fun.

Lindsay Porter

A Stitch Up

The aliens came it was a shock,
Space ships in the sky,
Pointed ears and dressed in green,
With one enormous eye.
They took us captive to their ship,
We could not wriggle free.
They held us trightly in their grip,
They really frightened me.
Pushing us on a staircase,
They started to move around,
Feeling sick and frightened,
We slowly left the ground.
Then in a flash we'd gone so fast,
We must have travelled far
When at last the staircase stopped,
I thought I saw a star,
Through a door the master came,
He made us take a seat,
And to our great surprise he said,
'How very nice to meet,
We need you earthlings for today
To teach us how to sew,
Gain us this experience and then we'll let you go.'
The tension was enormous
I grasped my chest in fright,
I could not sew a single stitch
Please help me through the night,
The fear in me took over
I let out a piercing scream,
Thankful to turn over,
And find it all a dream.

Renee Wallace

Baby Farming

Hello, I am your midwife today,
May I have your request form please
Do you have a trade in?
First time buyers, how lovely.
It was a male you ordered?
Male and white with blue eyes.
I'm afraid the computers are on the blink,
They've sent you an orange one.
No need to panic, I'll just send it back.
Can't have you getting the wrong one.
Might clash with the decor.
Here you are now dear,
One white male child,
I can just see him coming down
the birthing tunnel,
the instructions and receipts are in the bag
Bring him in for a service at about a year
Happy families.
Next.

Margaret Paterson

Our Planet

The whole world looks sad and grey
With violence persecution and fear each day,
We are governed by the upper classes
No justice for the working classes.
Mugging rape poverty and theft
Foreclosing mortgages and nothing left,
Hate misery hunger and tales of woe
Out on the street and nowhere to go.
No home no cash and job
For some it is hard to make a few bob,
But in the world every nation
Is coming to the end of civilisation.
Then the coming of the Lord
As he is sent
To establish a new and better government.
For the end of the world is growing near
So love each other and have no fear,
The time is coming for nations to put away their arms
And turn their weapons into plows and hoes,
To cultivate their farms.
So love each other and open the door,
To everlasting life forever more.

D E Collins

Captain's Log Book

Space, the final frontier,
Captains Log Book,
Contains information on the Star Ship Enterprise.

The Vulcan Mr Spock, Dr Spock, Captain Spock?
Joined the Enterprise some 10-15 light years ago,
And with one extra resident aboard,
Sci-fi adventure, may begin.

Strange explanations,
For Jupiter, or is it Saturn, or Mars?
A form of life dwells,
Beneath the reddish purple glow . . . It's Mars!

This wonderous ship,
A lady, like us,
Only she does not breath air,
She is the equal, equivalent to a thousand viper crafts.

Her power is immense,
And the lights,
The lights shine bright,
On this cosmetically gorgeous machine.

A thing of beauty is she,
The woman in the silver dress,
Encrusted in colourless sequins,
And she shall never die, the *Star Ship Enterprise.*

Emma Nielsen

Space Special Star Trek

Star Trek is an amazing series
Of which we never seem to weary,
Captain Kirk is a very brave man
He goes to places, where no man can.
His ship that's called, The Enterprise
Flies through endless space above the skies,
The adventures and horrors, the crew have survived
Its a wonder that any are still alive.
Spock the one who has no human reactions
Is by far, the one with lots of human attractions,
Scott the Engineer so clever and fine
Can beam you up to land on a dime.
The Doctor with his amazing tool
Does his job, always keeping his cool,
Uhura gazes into everlasting space
And tells them where next to chase.
Sulu a very important member of the crew
Steers the ship so surely and true.
The ship and brave men, seem to live forever more
And of this you can be very sure,
If in future space travel should arise
I would like to go on a ship called the Enterprise.

Winifred Arundel Smith

My Hero

I still love you Captain Kirk
Even though
Your bursting through your shirt.
I remember you Jim
Tall and handsome
Ever so slim, just a boy
With your sidekick Mr McCoy.
And the wonderous Mr Spock
Looking splendid in a frock
Stepping foot on unknown planets
Winning flights with lumps of granite.
Always the one to fall in love
With the goddesses up above,
Justice and peace were your mission.
I would like just one transmission
To the starship Enterprise,
There to gaze into your eyes
So beam me up Scotty.

E Thorpe

Astral Planes

When I was a capsule, out on the astral planes
My paralysing pistol would coagulate your veins -
And the knobs go flipping, and the signals pipping away.

I'm faster than the speed of light, I see what can't be seen;
I'll flip my knob and flash it on your atmospheric screen.

I'm lighter than a feather, I'm infinitely tall;
My footsteps set me flying like a gas-filled rubber ball.

Bespattered by the fragments of planetary soils,
Sometimes I feel I suffocate in Monty Python's coils.

There's an easy satellite rider - he's a friend to me and you.
Some people call him Quatermass, some call him Dr. Who.

The Moon it is my satellite, it's under my control.
I'll plant the flag, I'll call it mine - and dig another hole.

There is not a grain of truth in what we hear or see,
In concept's of magnitude, nor of velocity;
It's all governed by the principle of relativity.

The Mekon is a poppy-head, he's coloured mountain green,
How he floats upon his gravy boat like a glossy magazine.
When I was a capsule, out on the astral planes.
My paralysing pistol would coagulate your veins.
And the knobs go flipping, and the signals pipping away.

David Russell

Now I Know

I am the child,
My mothers to hold.

My mother deprived now,
Her parents tears.

Death becomes winsome life,
Faintly upon silvery breath.

The child to hold,
Transparent victories continue.

My parents tears gone,
For I am your mother.

Steven McLuckie

A Tribute to a Brave Dog

It was a wild and windy afternoon
As I sat to eat my lunch,
Outside the rain was pounding down
And a tree branch snapped with a crunch.

Then all of a sudden my dog stood up
His back and hackles raised,
He stalked into my dining room
Barking as though he was crazed.

I felt a shiver down my spine
My hands were clammy and cold,
I wondered if it would be wise
If the local Police were told.

But my dog came back and barked again
His big white teeth were bared,
I decided I'd better follow him
Even though I was very scared.

So I followed him through to the other room -
Then smiled and called his name,
For my brave little dog was telling me
There was a wasp on the window pane!

Joyce Lightfoot

Deep In Space

Deep in space my heart lies
I was born out of time
My mind is a computer
I feel its such a crime,
That when space age really comes
There will be nothing I can do,
but hopefully I will re-enter
and appear on Dr Who.

Ada Goodworth

First Footing Ceannaichean

Three thousand feet above the glen
Ceannaichean's cairn was my high altar
On that January day,
A mound of sacred stone
Sanctified by incense mists
And wild, winnowing wind.

My storm-worn hassock
Had endured a million years
Of eternity -
An eternity that's forever now
In the vast cathedrals
Of our metamorphic hills;
Mountains are forever.

Centuries may roll, but
The sculptured crags of Choinnich
Will still beckon
Across the Pollan Buidhe,
Lofty Liathach will yet
Thrust her gashed pinnacles
Into the Eagle blue,

The congregation of deer
Will forever browse
And bend a reverent knee
On the green lawns of Coire Lair
Whilst high on Beinn Liath Mhor
Ptarmigan, white as winter,
Will croak their bass Amens
To the hill man's scattered prayers.

Gordon Booth

Star Trek

I am the Enterprise,
Space Invader,
Speeding
Through paths of far flung stars.
My captain is Kirk,
Controller of decisions,
Guardian of the crew.
Spock, creature of intellect,
Bones, man of medicine,
Scottie, of engineering prowess,
All subservient to him.
And he . . . to me!
Together,
We explore new frontiers,
See soul shattering sights,
Hear alien sounds,
Feel wonder, mystery.
Taste, touch strange things.
Together,
We tremble on an abyss of discovery,
Man and technology combined.

Nesta Wilson

No Phoenix

Tongues of fire
Produced the heated words,
Licking, sinuous and probing
Searing the soft membranes of our mind -
White heated sparks spit out and sting,
Prick with hot needle tips
The surface of the soul.
Wounding and hurting:
Death by a thousand words.

Grey smoke slowly chokes the reasoned voice,
Surrounds us with a blanket of despair,
Blurs shapes which were so sharply honed together,
Clouds dullard eyes
Unable, now, to see
        the right from wrong.

Too late, the fire is dying.
No fuel left to feed the hate-filled flame.
Hard chill usurps the heat of passion.
Ash stifles fragile, nascent hope.

Write, blackly, on the empty hearth
Our epitaph -

        Here was a happy home,
        And we were lovers, once.

Hazel Smith

The Questions?

The sky above holds the mysterious of the heavens.
the sun and moon are the guardians of time.
And mans ceaseless search is to help all humanity
As we live through disasters of each Words decline.

Earthquakes, calamities, they all come our way,
And tragedy from wars leave sorrowful days.
Yet 'in an ideal world life should be good
If communication between people were understood,
Greed, and demand would be no more.
And peace and harmony would be restored.
No colour bar or different creed of Jews
Muslim, or of Christian belief.

The Universe would be as in the beginning,
Mysterious, Timeless, ageless living.
No conquest for the Earth would man pursue.
For you can't own the Earth.
Tis
The Earth that owns you.

Mollie Clarke

Space 1999

'Tis not just the eyes of the moon filled with tears,
Many hearts share the tragedy of loss.
Many souls speak of grief in a crowd all alone,
'Tis the loneliness woven on each cross.
No earth can they see, no orb dressed in life,
Only emptiness ebbs within the dark.
Gone are the trees, rivers, mountains and seas,
Buried 'neath the tears of grieving hearts.

Once the earth had a moon, 'twas her child she would croon,
Oblivious to mans incessant wars.
Mankind meddled with God tearing the child from its home,
Leaving only a silent tideless shore.

Torn from her grasp ran the cold smiling mask,
Where no one can hear the tortured cry.
The moon drives on alone upon a never ending road
And the stars are the lamp posts in her sky.

The moon is their berth, their hearts still on earth,
But all they could see was their shrine.
They pray to their Gods with the vows of the moon,
Remembering space 1999.

David Bridgewater

The Travelling Show

The exciting mind I now live in
Could it be classed as sin,
The day may never return
Different views, the need to learn.
The walls begin their breathing
Paranoid, quick I'm leaving
Can't escape this slow picture
Emotions caught in splendid mixture,
the freezing air makes me sweat
Rising higher, nothing is set.
Tonight I'm in love with myself
Weird scenes come in their wealth.
This is my own travelling show
Easy, then hard to control.
Still working, still going strong
Dawn arrives, for sleep I long.

Dean Haith

The Final Frontier

The Final Frontier of endless size
Beckons Earth's Federation Starship Enterprise,
Life, but not as we know it Jim,
Another adventure's about to begin.

Scotty, when will our Warp Engines work,
Almost ready Captain Kirk,
Mr. Spock, what do you see,
Another life form Captain, but it's new to me.

First Officer Sulu, have you mapped our way,
We should have left yesterday,
Captain Sir, you may not have known,
We'll have to cross the Neutural Zone.

The Romulans are a Warlike Race,
They don't allow anyone to infringe their Space,
We will have to pass their Outpost Station,
There is no choice, orders are from the Federation.

The Klingons may present a problem too,
Then Mr. Sulu, we will have to show them what we can do,
Uhura, have you made contact yet,
Sorry Captain, too much interference on my set.

Keep all channels open then,
And relay the message, once again,
Mr. Chekov, are you ready,
Yes Captain Sir, I've got the helm nice and steady.

Startreks crew, representing the Human Race,
Twenty Third Century Man, shows a more compassionate face,
Intrepid Enterprise Crew, seek and find,
To the benefit of all Mankind.

Jim Wilson

V

V is for Visitor,
a stranger to our earth.
They arrive in giant spaceships,
proclaiming peace and friendship,
and to tell us of their worth.
We trust them for a while,
as they treat us kind and smile.
They have a human face,
but we no nothing of their race.
They're taking over slowly,
it's time to we put them in their place.
Terror campaigns and propaganda,
fill us with depression.
We must fight and overcome,
this sinister alien oppression.
Our fighting tears their skin.
But their no humans,
for underneath their disguise,
is slimy, green, reptilian skin.
Now we no their not here for peace,
because they haven't been that shrewd.
But we learn,
their here to take the Water,
and us as well, for food.
The human race will perish and die,
as reptilian armies gather us like sheep.
They are stronger than us,
to the Visitor's, we've suffered a deadly defeat . . .

David Wesley Cooper

When the Space Travellers Came to Dinner

An Alien ship fell on the Tardis, there was an almighty *crash!*
The leader looked like a robot, his arms - like knives - what a *smash*!
It was then that the Daleks - who had been smuggled aboard,
Began the assault on the aliens, fighting until they were floored.
A shout gave out, the aliens, then the daleks stopped too,
A voice said, 'Captain Kirk here - where is Dr Who?'
Old Scottie had beamed him down, the aliens stood aside,
The daleks confirmed, they'd just gone along for the ride!
'We've come along for that meal,' said Kirk, 'that *Who* invited us to.'
'We've got plenty,' the aliens said, ' - will packet potato do?'
At that, Dr Who appeared, his scarf almost down to the ground,
Five of him appeared simultaneously, 'til only one was found.
'We're here for the big celebration,' said Kirk, 'thirty years to the day.'
Everyone there agreed for peace on Dr Who's *Anniversary!*

Judith Lonie

March of Progress

The corrugated fields lap amongst the
Legs of the metallic giants,
Linked together by loose chains,
Their four legs move them on.
The curving tarmac of the shore watches,
As the waves rise in fury,
Swaying in the sea - one giant stumbles,
Metal crumbling into the ocean,
Blinding bolts of angered fury,
Light up the ravished sea,
Creatures on the shore ignore this,
Dashing back and forth - glowing satisfaction.

I Burnley

Above the Clouds

A life in space, way above the clouds,
Gazing at the stars, shining so proud.
the enchanting moon, a step away,
Day trips to mars, on the shuttle -
Most dry days.

Aboard the enterprise, everything is new,
Instead of eating meals, only tablets will do.
Spock is oh so logical, Kirk is never dull,
Scotty always grumpy, his workload always full.

Me, I'm just a cog, a small piece of the works,
Checking that the space suits fit, but floating has it's perks.
I test all the equipment, where gravity has no weight,
Just drifting aimlessly, helplessly, peacefully, to every crater gate.

Tranquillity is spoilt, by frequent klingon attacks,
But the crew pull together, lasers send them back.
Tomorrow is observing day, planet Venus is unknown,
Everything here is fascinating, always being flown.

C Griffiths

Ode To Star Trek

Beam me up Scottie, that's now a joke
Up he goes in a puff of smoke
Graphics are magic and anything goes
Someone designs those wonderful clothes.

When celestial beings give them some stick
They're vaporised quickly at the flick of a switch
Spock is no mortal, he has pointed ears
His body won't age, he'll go on for years.

The Captain is Kirk, as people will know
He's ready to go where no others will go
He won't stand invaders who're bent on attack
If they give aggression, they soon get it back.

A touch of romance creeps in now and then
Females around make a change for the men
The ship *Enterprise* beats all the rest
To conquer the world you must have the best.

Doreen Gardner

Space Travel

Beam me up it's time to dash,
Move to warp, before we crash.

The Klingons are now out of sight,
But Spock knows, it's not quiet right.

It's time to go where no man has boldly gone before,
We never know what is in store.

Will it be green, or barren waste?
Will we be welcome, or kicked out in haste?

Well, Phazers at ready, says James T Kirk,
No time to talk, and get rid of that smirk.

For time and space waits for no man, they say,
So beam us down, to start a new day.

K L B Drury

The Void

A vast emptiness across the void, so unreal.
Where all is relative, so unreal.
The occasional atom uselessly employed
may cluster locally surreal.

A denseness is created that attracts,
all conform to a spherical norm.
So regular are such, it distracts
from the possibility of alternative form.

Position, speed, acceleration, density,
are relative to past and actual comparison.
Laws meet this end in authenticity,
satisfying happenings until new may jettison.

Upon this density in a minute corner
atomshave neighboured for consciousness.
Whether by pattern or a random deformer
the question burns within that consciousness.

A minuteness of undefined emptiness.
Charges in opposition rotate in absence.
This emptiness gathers into a solidiness,
an actualness that satisfies the conscience.

Complex worlds evolve from simplistic construction,
worlds of solidarity that support abstract thought.
Where all *that is* can be in speculation
never knowing yet asking what ought.

All is mostly nothing.
Even its' most dense composition.
Are we therefore as nothing,
good enough reason for our disposition.

M G Bradley

A Trekky Business

Her bun's untouched, the tea is stewed,
And Violet's mother sighs . . .
. . . her daughter used to love her food
. . . those cream cakes, jams and pies.
But Violet's eyes are glued elsewhere -
To her favourite *Star Trek comics*
With Captain Picard, Bev and Riker.
She ignores the gastronomics.
'Oh Violet, please eat up your bun
And wash your hands and face.'
'I haven't got time for that Mum,
I'm due in outer space.'
'Oh no you're not, you need new shoes,
And we're both going shopping.'
(but Violet's booked on the next space cruise,
for a spot of planet - hopping)
And tho' she makes it into town
And attempts to be dutifully shod
She disappears when Mum turns round . . .
'Oy . . . who d'you think you are . . . God?'
But Violet cannot hear this
And starts to re materialise
In the home that's where her heart is
The star ship *Enterprise.*
Mum wrings her hands, shouts and cries
'That girl is driving me potty.'
Beseechingly, she turns to the skies,
'Please beam us all up Scotty.'

Julie Humphries

Them

Looking out of the window
There they were looking in
menacingly at me,
Shivers ran through my spine,
Don't be silly Hilda,
They're only bloody street lamps!
I surmised.

Can't forget that film,
War of the Worlds,
H G Wells and all that stuff,
Frightening creatures from nowhere,
I remember they came clickety-click,
Along the High Street,
Their wings were made of steel,
As they flew, their tiny, swan-like heads,
looked in every nook and cranny,
for humans to kill.
One fire-like blast and finito you were no more!

They came and peeked into the church,
Their eyes merciless as yet, they saw
the vicar and his people, kneel down *as one*,
To pray to their God for deliverance,
No help came for them the creatures
Sent forth their evil ray.
Then flew on and on to conquer new
cities, new town, until only *them* remained.

H G Hutchin

Star Trek

Imagine a ship that can travel through space,
amongst the stars and the planets, amongst any race.
The USS Enterprise is one very such thing,
it holds all sorts of life forms and has machines that can sing!

They can beam down to land wherever they choose,
sometimes they gain knowledge, sometimes they lose.
All sorts of planets lie in wait to be found,
the ship's crew explore them, feet firm on the ground.

Such mysterious places are both intriguing and grand,
no wonder comparatively, our Earth seems so bland.
Not all of the planets though are happy and *sunny*.
Some house weird people who are vicious and cunning.

The Enterprise crew are trained to perfection,
so an encounter with evil means they can fight for protection.
their Starship is equipped with everything they'd desire,
they have lasers and shields, a holodeck and phaser.

Their Captain, a well mannered and respected man,
treats them all fairly, like a Scotsman his clan.
Although the crew's varied, with humans and rarities
They get along fine without taking liberties.

Yet however weird their lifestyle's may seem,
they all work together, a united team!
Perhaps this is why the Starship Enterprise continues,
to visit all planets and far away venues.

Carol Ross